TO RECONNOITER THE TERRITORIES OF
BRAIN, MIND, AND PHILOSOPHY

R. Garner Brasseur, M.D.

authorHOUSE®

AuthorHouse™
1663 Liberty Drive
Bloomington, IN 47403
www.authorhouse.com
Phone: 1 (800) 839-8640

Published by AuthorHouse   09/15/2016

ISBN: 978-1-5246-3959-4 (sc)
ISBN: 978-1-5246-3958-7 (e)

Library of Congress Control Number: 2016915195

Print information available on the last page.

Any people depicted in stock imagery provided by Thinkstock are models, and such images are being used for illustrative purposes only. Certain stock imagery © Thinkstock.

This book is printed on acid-free paper.

Table of Contents

On Consciousness

On Memory

Anatomy and Physiology of CNS

Nature of Nature

Ponder These Matters

Dreaming Up Utopia

Persistent Uncertainty

But Life Goes On

Foreword

It seems to me appropriate in my waning years to gather up my modest final thoughts on the ancient subject of Philosophy. Philosophy being a product of the enigmatic nature of consciousness and the mysterious mind of man it would seem remiss of me to neglect to probe also into that as a part of this little essay.

And as human consciousness and the mind are products of the neurons, flesh, and blood of the brain, it seems obvious to me that Brain, Mind, and Philosophy fit naturally together as a topic for a little thesis. And thus it is that I thought to reconnoiter the territories of Brain, Mind, and Philosophy.

I fancy that I have been somewhat enlightened by the time and effort that has gone into the project. Hopefully, a few readers may find it interesting and informative.

R. Garner Brasseur. M.D.

In The Beginning

"Our most advanced thinking can be effectively and reliably evaluated only on paper. The thought we set down in writing, thereby reveals defects that would otherwise escape correction." (p. 305 *Out of Chaos*)

❋　❋　❋　❋　❋

Foundational Ideas

In ancient times Cratylus (5th century B.C.) was among the first to emphasize that all-everything, and everybody are in a state of continual change. That even words change their meanings and language is in a state of continual flux. We have never any certainty that we are communicating with one another accurately. (see Abel) The only universal principle is that everything changes-that alone remains unaltered. (p. 71 Popkin) "It is the distinct mark of a philosophical question that it cannot be put, or weighed, or answered without bringing into play and without reference to all that is", says Josef Pieper.

Idealism refers to the existence of intangible mind, the existence of which is thought to account for all that there is in the world. "It takes as the fundamental and irreducible feature of the universe the existence of mind in the universal sense. Its versions unfortunately deprecate the commonsense world of material things." (p. 2 Abel)

Absolute idealism. The world seen as an indivisible whole and each part is what it is because of its place in the ideal whole. Russell denounced this, and says, "I think the universe is all spot and jumps, without unity or continuity or coherence or orderliness or any of the other properties that governs love."

Hegel's absolute idealism is the view that 'spirit' alone (in the sense of self conscious thought) is real. (p. 103 John E. Smith)

Materialism and Idealism are both monistic metaphysical theories-in the suggestion that there is only one kind of thing in the world. Materialism refers to the physical and tangible self, the world, and universe in which we exist. The theory that the motion of matter can in principle account for all that there is in the world.

Philosophical Materialism-the postulate that matter is the stuff of all existence and that all mental and spiritual phenomena are its by-products. In short, that mind is a product of brains.

Spinoza (a monist, rather than a dualist) says there is only one reality, but it has two attributes, namely thought and extension. (p. 201 Abel) Neither are the processes of mind something which can be seen or touched.

Monism suggests that only one of the two categories exists (Intangible mind, or tangible matter).

Naturalism intends the single category of Nature to encompass all that exists in space and time-organic, inorganic, and intangible.

Mechanism sees the world as a huge clockwork that is entirely and uniquely determined by its component parts and the interactions thereof. It adds to materialism the hypothesis of determinism. It would seem to exclude the matters of uncertainty and probably of Quantum Mechanics.

Determinism and chance. Determinism says that all events have causes connected by general laws. The concept of cause is basic to determinism. Yet we do not ever observe one external event compelling another event to happen by necessity. We never see any glue connecting events. We oft have seen what happens when one billiard ball strikes another. An infant might have been taken with the regularity of it. It is only the regularity with which we see it that convinces us of some underlying cause. We might have as apt to have seen the one or the other to explode. The cause of planetary motion was even more mystifying. How could one planet act upon another across such vast distances.

Determinism is much too valuable a postulate to abandon. But it denies that there is any such thing as chance. "As soon as man encounters turbulence, he gives up determinism"-Tolstoy

As to what there is in the world, there is a division into things and events. A pen is a thing (substance) and occupies time and space. A discussion is an event and runs through time (a process) or happens in time but does not have extension.

<u>Form</u>-The essential nature of a thing as distinguished from the matter in which it is embedded. The preexisting idea of which all actual things are copies.

<u>Idea</u>-The conception of a thing existing before anything of its kind was created or made; the original pattern of which all actual things of the same sort are but imperfect copies.

Perception vs. Reality

Yes, there is but a loose fit between the 'mind' and the world. Nobody can be sure that what he believes is exactly correct. Which seems to be part of the explanation as to why man is a natural explorer. Naturally driven also into pursuit of satisfactions and avoidance or elimination of pain, dissatisfactions, and un-pleasantries.

Philosophical questions and riddles sometimes have no solution at all, which is part of what one means by "a **loose fit between 'mind' and the world**". (p. xxiv Abel)

✳   ✳   ✳   ✳   ✳

Creation History

The growth of knowledge has permitted many simplifications or reductions in the field of Philosophy. 'Caloric' was once supposed to be the independent essence or principle of heat, but has been reduced to the motion of molecules. The gene as the unit of heredity has been reduced to the chemical DNA etc. (p.4 Abel)

Though our science has made commendable and useful progress since the Renaissance and the time of Francis Bacon, we may expect that the time will never arrive when it will complete the enlightenment of mankind.

The history of the universe might be said to be punctuated by a series of highly significant great leaps forward. I have come to ponder briefly the BIG HISTORY sequence of fortuitous developments in the history of the world:

- Creation or the big bang which are both highly speculative → Primordial Plasma
- Cooling of cosmic plasma into molecules.
- 2 or 3 star generations produce increasingly the ever heavier types of molecules.
- Evolving solar systems produces a rare occasional 'goldilocks' planet.
- Accumulation of water, air, oxygen on the 'goldilocks' earth.
- The emergence of the first life on earth as one-celled organisms and its evolution into ever more advanced multi-cellular creatures and beasts. A dialectical process.
- The evolution of creatures with CNS "minds".

- Death of dinosaurs and making room for mammalian species.
- Arrival of primates as a step preceding Mankind.
- Nakedness of man on the killing fields of Serengeti. His motivation to improve his situation.
- The beginnings of language and use of fire.
- Arrival of agriculture and life in villages.
- The evolution by man into cities and civilizations.
- Horsepower to alleviate the drain on human time and energy.
- 5,000 years of human competition, contest, and war to spur innovation to civilized mankind.
- Writing, printing to facilitate memory and language.
- The invention of the Guttenberg Press.
- Education of the masses.
- Steam Engine to greatly enlarge energy to production.
- Mass production to produce food and creature comforts.
- Accumulation of information.
- The now evolving age of electronic computerization and world-wide communication.

It is said that one hundred billion persons have been born to this earth. Of which, seven billion currently exist alive.

Contributors To Information

Eventually the opening of the mind made possible the opening of the seaways and the discovery of the New World. Imagine the astonishment of that. And other astonishments were soon to follow.

In our times it seems difficult to believe how slow and belatedly mankind had come to perceive the geography of the world through the explorations of Marco Polo, the Portuguese, Columbus, Cortez, Magellan, Pizzaro, Lewis and Clark, Humboldt, Livingston, and Stanley.

Leeuwenhoek astonished the world with his discovery of an entire miniature population of microscopic creatures with which we more macroscopic types unbenouncedly share our daily and intimate existence. Microscopic creatures that bring far more disease and death to human lives than the predators of Serengeti and the Jungles of this world.

Such persons as Galileo, Kepler, Newton, Einstein, and Boehr have expanded our perceptions of Astronomy and introduced mankind to an Immensely Wide Universe.

Hutton, and Wegener, have introduced us to Geology, Continental Drift and the structure of the earth.

Schleeman, Darwin, Wallace, and Leeky, have dug into the earth to make us aware of the prehistory of life, mankind, and bygone civilizations. We begin to envision a law of progress of humanity which suggests the high antiquity of Man (lessons of archaeology); and in paleontology, we note a cabal of similar development.

Priestly, LaVoisier, Mendeleyev, Boyle, Rutherford, and Curry, have deduced to us some conceptual information and organization of atoms and molecules far beyond our limited unaided perceptions.

Newton, Copernicus, Galileo, Kepler, Einstein, Boehr, Hawking, and Sagan have acquainted us with the Cosmos. Newton, Daves, Faraday, Maxwell, Marconi, and Edison have acquainted and analyzed for our use the subject material of electromagnetism and field theory.

Electro-magnetism cannot be explained mechanically at all.

From *Music of The Spheres* it is suggested that on a log scale of all entities known to exist, the physical structure of a mortal human being lies somewhere about the middle, between the extremely tiny such as an atom-to that of the extremely large, i.e. the universe in totality. (see Murchie)

The function and nature of the brain seems as though to mediate and coordinate our being between the tangible realities of the world and the intangible uncertainties and possibilities of the quantum and conceptual worlds. One cannot exclude the intangible mind as an explanatory principle of human nature. Mind may be even an explanatory principle as to cause and function of the universe.

✳　✳　✳　✳　✳

Stardust And Information

Immediately subsequent to the 'big bang', elementary particles precipitate into rudimentary Hydrogen from the chaotic plasma as it cools. Hydrogen coalesces into stars. Within the star, Hydrogen atoms interact, fuse, and evolve one-by-one into first-order molecules in space, under the influence of heat and pressure through time and process. A process which when completed ends in the violent explosive 'death' of a star. An explosion which produces such excessive energy as to bring into existence (again, by fusion) the second-order of ever enlarging atoms (those with a molecular weight beyond that of iron) flung widely into the void, and from whence condense second generation stars and globs of assorted molecular debris of various size including dust and even the occasional planetary size globs of matter-such as the planets of our own solar system.

Information imbedded in the universe would appear to be ever in the process of communication among the tangible aspects of the universe. Every elementary particle seems as though to be imbued with information as to how it may or may not interact with every other particle and molecule in accordance with the laws of nature. We mortal earth-bound sentinels are entangled with the particles and elements of the universe and likewise entangled, constrained, and enabled by the same laws of nature. The every element of each of our physical existences is an intimate part of the immense universe-each, a bit of the stardust of the universe

It has been demonstrated that the mass of each atom is almost entirely to be found in its nucleus. And that there is a vast void by which the nucleus is separated from its orbiting electrons. Since each mortal being is composed of atoms, it follows that our bodies are likewise each a vast emptiness, though our perceptions are far too gross to directly perceive that reality. A vast stream of cosmic rays, neutrinos and elementary particles from the cosmos continuously pierces through the substance of every tangible object and each person. Only rarely does one such proton in the cosmic stream encounter or shatter a single proton in one's entire body. An imperceptible event of rarely any consequence. Yet so massive and continuous is the flux of cosmic rays, that the cumulative insult through time, does cause some ever ongoing genetic change and some disease process in the occasional person.

There would appear to be in our universe an inert material of atoms and molecules which is said to be quite different and separate in nature from that which contains 'life'-plants and animals. But we can as well take a wider view of the nature of that-which-is. In recent centuries we have come to understand that even the lowliest of atoms is 'alive' with activity and movement. All of which interact or fail to interact with one another on the basis of individual properties as prescribed in the laws of nature. The very electrons rapidly and continuously orbit the nucleus of each and every atom. And these electrons spin up or down or left or right. Where do they get their energy?

Some are wont to say that electrons, like the quanta of light beams are themselves packets of energy. And point out that the atoms too are constantly in motion. And it might also be said, that the very void is 'alive' with the intangible relevance of uncertainty, possibility, and probability. The distinction then between 'inert matter' and what we name as 'life' begins to blur. What we are accustomed then to name as 'life' is, perhaps an overly restrictive definition?

We mortals tend to cling desperately to our mortality and are troubled to have to ponder the inevitability of our demise. Once we concede the ever present immaterial abstraction of 'the-eternal-**Why**' which is forever on one's mind, we who abide here in the presence of the-something (That Which Is) are confronted with <u>the fundamental question of the existence (of anything). Why is there something instead of nothing</u>? For of the two, 'the-nothing' strikes me as the more rational possibility. But it is my view that the two are co-existent. That there could not be a-nothing without a-something: nor a-something without a-nothing. For each would require the other by way of a comparison. We who abide as substantive sentient beings here in 'the-something' are, ourselves, a-something that has been derived both from the-nothing and the-something by a cause (parents-within the-something) where we currently abide. But that we too (as 'mind' and body) are individually destined to return to the realm of non-existent entities while the atoms and molecules of our physical body are returned to once more recycle into the stardust from which they have derived.

From my point of view in the here-and-now, one can say that if there ever had been an all encompassing nothingness, yet one must conclude that the nothingness had the potential of giving rise to a-something. Giving rise namely to the universe in which we currently abide. And that the universe we now inhabit appears to be a continuously evolving and changing universe.

Yes, any primordial and complete nothingness would seem to be a simpler and logically a more likely alternative than a-something in which we now have our mortal existence. A dilemma for our contemplation and amusement.

✳   ✳   ✳   ✳   ✳

Monistic vitalism posits monism rather than dualism. Meaning that there is only one "essence" that constitutes life and matter at a fundamental level. It seems to agree along with Spinoza that spirit and matter are separate components, but that they as two aspects of the one fundamental reality. As an individual coin has two aspects, heads and tails. That the physical and the metaphysical are everywhere conjoined. And that the two never exist except in combination with one another. That even what is thought of as 'inert matter' does, in fact have life. That even within each molecule and individual atom there is life, in that each has a continuous motion within themselves, and each is imbued with the metaphysical knowledge that informs them of how they may or may not respond or interact with one another. So it is with human beings, each has both a physical and a metaphysical component.

Scientists have been said to be unable to demonstrate that plants and animals can have had their origins in so-called 'inert' matter. But that now seems perhaps to be untrue. About 1949, Urey and Miller had synthesized amino acids-the building blocks of life-in a laboratory. And we have become aware that amino acids occur naturally in this universe. We mere mortals are in fact composed entirely of these supposedly 'inert' atoms in the molecules of our substance. And we recently have word that the researches of Craig Venture are on the verge of the generation of a primitive 'life form' from such 'inert matter'.

❊   ❊   ❊   ❊   ❊

Science is but one of mankind's attempts to probe the vastness of our ignorance of the life, the world, and the universe of which we are a part (and in which we are immersed). Philosophy along with religions are (in common with science) two earlier and additional probes into the vast unknown. Life itself perhaps, is but a probe of nature into the universe from which it is derived. The every probe and investigation begins with doubt and curiosity. One might charitably suppose that there be some initial honesty of intent in the speculations and study of each (religion, philosophy, science, and life). All, appear to us to have had their origins in immemorial times past. Each of these probes is a long and complex study that has occupied the scanty idle time available to the minds of men through innumerable consecutive generations. It does not seem unreasonable to suppose that those ongoing quests (themselves) are an evidence that implies that none have yet achieved its goal of providing definite nor fully satisfactory answers. Who among us has not dabbled somewhat with the methods and theories of each?

Issues and Suspicions

Berlinski On Delusion

From Berlinski's, book "*The Devils Delusion*"
(abstract and commentary by RGB)

"Argument follows from assumptions. And assumptions follow from beliefs. Very rarely-perhaps never-do beliefs reflect an agenda determined entirely by facts." (p. 103 Berlinski)

Through the ages arises contest, claim, and counterclaim among the advocates of each probe-as well as rivalry for dominance among the probes. None of our probes into the nature, origin, or purpose of life, in this world and universe has successfully completed its mission. Meanwhile, the vast majority of mankind live out their lives with never any much regard for the tentative conclusions of any such theories. The individual life is far too occupied with the sustainment of its life and its incessant dilemmas. Every avenue of probe is perhaps of some variable use or some consolation to every life. Consolations which are duly taxed to add to mankind's every burden of life.

The book's author indicates that he himself leans toward atheism. But the theme of the book and its tone seems highly prejudicial toward a belief in God with emphasis on there being at least a possibility of some validity in creationism. So much so that one may well suspect that the author's foremost purpose is to garner a stream of personal income from the fundamentalist creationists that will lap up his apologetics. He in fact says he has written the book to assuage the frustrations of creationists and the religiously inclined.

The construction of Berlinski's book is elitist in style, burgeoning with a repertoire of complex words such as to impress its fundamentalist readers who will delight in his long incomprehensible sentences. Something as incomprehensible as is a necessity of science to coin words and allegories by which to fully express the complexity of the advanced calculus which but few mortals have had time, or cause to attempt a comprehension.

In truth of course, but few of we ordinary citizens can grasp the complexity of intricate cosmology or the calculus by which the speculative sciences attempt to explain and justify the ongoing string theories with their innumerable invisible dimensions, the implausible multi-verses, and the evolving theories of subatomic particles upon which they speculate.

As the author rightly concludes, neither the notion of God nor the theory of the big bang are adequate explanations of either the cause or the purpose of the universe. But he is especially severe in his putting down what he perceives to be scientific hubris and elitism with which he takes issue. And to make light of the men and women of science, and their remarkable achievements.

But the reality as I see it, is that science has contributed considerably more towards the material quality of life of modern man than has either religion or philosophy. Consider after all the tenuous situation of our hominid ancestors upon the savannas of Africa compared to the relative ease and comfort of our own lives in peaceful times in the USA. And consider our much increased longevity and generally good health. Consider the security, and warmth of shelter which we enjoy. Consider the regular supply of edible food and the abundance of clean water which are a part of our lives in these United States of America in the twenty-first century.

Far be it from me to suggest or propose that the yearnings and curiosities of we mere mortals for understanding and comprehension are either vain or pointless. Einstein says science without religion is lame. And that religion without science is blind. Each new intellectual theory (metaphysical or scientific) can be said to be at least an evidence of the heroic aspirations of individual beings to advance against the mighty obstacle of the great unknown even in the face of our mortal intellectual limitations. Ought one better to put forth one's intellectual efforts(?) or continue merely to promulgate, devise, and prolong the mystic and ritual in the vain hope and expectation on tired prayer-bones for revelation from above?

✻ ✻ ✻ ✻ ✻

Kierkegaard Downgrade

Kierkegaard, **(1813-1855),** unlike Socrates, wants instead to suppose that the learner does not have this knowledge pre-positioned within himself and no way to acquire knowledge. Has in fact no valid knowledge and therefore no way of recognizing a truth even when he encounters such. Completely unable to distinguish a truth from and an untruth. Kierkegaard wants to suggest that there occurs 'a miracle' of enlightenment within his hypothetical individual such as to have removed his previous ignorance. If the miracle had been precipitated upon one (i.e. by God) without one's having (unknowingly) desired, it would not be a significant event in his life. To make this moment of enlightenment decisive to the course of a man's life, that man must have had to desire his transformation into enlightenment-without his own person knowing that (A hint that K. is wanting to establish his conception of man's mystical 'soul', or 'inner man'). In addition, (according to Kierkegaard) <u>that moment is decisive</u> in the man's life, for he is thereafter a completely changed man. And thereafter this enlightenment is eternal knowledge within his being. One must suppose that Kierkegaard has in mind something like unto the phenomenon of a Billy Graham evangelical grand slam.

God, like the king in Kierkegaard's story has created a situation in which He (God) is unrecognizable so that human beings will believe in Him through faith alone. "One must not count too much on God. But, perhaps God counts on us...". It seems likely that he has picked up that concept (salvation by faith alone) from Martin Luther's main religious doctrine.

"Everything we experience is temporal and changing, and hence (by definition) not God,-since God is said to be eternal and unchanging" according to those who invented Him and the Theology which has taken up that cause. But these qualities of God are purely hypothetical notions; and based on mere dogma from arbitrary concepts of assertion of early synagogue and church fathers. (p.188 Popkin)

So much then for Kierkegaard. He is plainly more into theology, rather than philosophy. He is suggesting that "human beings of and by themselves are incapable of knowing anything that is certain, and that only through some sort of miraculous event intruded into their lives can they ever acquire such knowledge." Complete skepticism concerning mere mortal knowledge. Wants to suggest that we can only escape our tragic plight by blindly seeking a way out through faith alone. And that each person would have to find the solution in his own way. But, says he: "hope and desire are never wanting; desire leads the way, and hope follows."

Remember though, "They (hope and desire) do men the greatest harm. Concealed in their minds, they prevail over dangers that are plain to see." (from Thucydides' *Peloponnesian Wars*)

✳   ✳   ✳   ✳   ✳

Prayer And Religion

Needs, dependency, hopes, wishes, desires, and expectations, are with us from the inception of our lives. We learn to pray (ask of) with some success to those about us who are invested in our well being. We depend upon their affirmative response which at times is immediate, but oft delayed by limitations of reality and deficiency of their assets. We are often put off with "ask your mother" or "perhaps tomorrow" or "can't be done" or "another time". Where others can't, don't, or will not serve, we are inclined to learn to serve ourselves. We are tempted to believe that a letter to Santa Claus can sometimes succeed-or a prayer to the man in the great beyond. Wishful thinking becomes a part of our hope and aspiration but we must eventually learn and practice some self-discipline and personal initiative-to satisfy our own hopes. The last resort for much of what we need and desire is often beyond us. And this then oft enters into prayers to the man upstairs and one's hopes that he exists, and that perhaps he hears-and even at times responds. Religion of some form and variable depth always tempts a part of every man's psyche.

In the scheme of things, I am tempted to suppose that superstition and religions were first to evolve from early man's ignorance and natural curiosities. And that ongoing ignorance, curiosity, language, and religion gradually evolved into Philosophy. And that finally, merely rhetorical Philosophy motivated mankind to systematic observations and experimentation which were called forth by the urgent necessities of competition, contest, and warfare to produce the beginnings of Science.

❋   ❋   ❋   ❋   ❋

Wittgenstein Suggests

Wittgenstein from the 1930s has become much influential in contemporary philosophy through his connection to and influence at Cambridge and Oxford. My own impression-along with his-is that "Philosophical perplexity arises from certain rather subtle misuses of everyday languages." (p. 185 Popkin)

Words are intended to possess established meanings and uses. If we do not maintain some fixity of meaning in our discourse, communication (even with ourselves) becomes ever more difficult (p. 43 of Abel) Surely the accuracy of our intercommunications ought to benefit when we can clarify thought by definitive language.

We note in Roget's Thesaurus for example that the word **SOUL**, in actual usage, refers to (among other synonyms): body, ghost, spirit, a living soul, shadow, phantom, umbra, character, creature, being, human being, individual, man, mortal, person, personage.

There is plenty of additional cause for mis-communication between the deep thinkers of times past and present. Through the millennia, generation after generation of philosophers have used their own separate languages and peculiar words and expressions of ideas which all contribute to the confusions and misunderstanding between their various philosophies.

A variety of idiomatic meanings and expressions such as to suggest that there is ample cause for philosophies and philosophers to misunderstand one another and to leave considerable confusion in the subject of Philosophy down through the millennia and across various idiomatic languages with ongoing changes in the definitions of words. Besides the mater of definitions there is also the reality of connotations of words.

A poem by John Godfrey Saxs tells us of six wise-men (all were blind) who went to discover what an elephant was like. Each of the blind men touched a different part of the elephant's anatomy and came each to a different conclusion as to what was an elephant like.

. . . .
"Though each of them was partly right
Yet all were in the wrong!"

The poets conclusion was that:
"So oft in theological wars
The disputants...",
. . . .
And prate about an elephant
Not one of them has seen!"

✳ ✳ ✳ ✳ ✳

Wittgenstein informs us that the search for a perfect language which accurately mirrors the world can not be realized. What we learn of Wittgenstein is mostly indirect, through the paraphrasing of those much under his influence. I came across the work of his student (Gilbert Ryle, *The Concept of Mind*) in 1973. He points out that ordinary folks as well as philosophers have each a certain theory about the nature of the mind. Theories which are riddled with difficulties and often untenable.

Along with Ryle, I too have long since given up the notion of what has been thought of as "the-ghost-in-the-machine", i.e. the notion (from Descartes) of a separate but intangible entity within our skulls that is variously designated as a separate loose entity such as 'the spirit', or 'the soul'.

[I continue to use the term 'mind' throughout the entirety of this book. But I use it with the clear implication and understanding that the 'mind' is but a function of the brain or CNS-not a separate entity from the brain. And that the word 'mind', is not to be considered as interchangeable with words such as 'soul', or 'spirit', for example.]

Terms such as 'knowing', 'believing', 'feeling', 'inferring', 'doubting', etc. do not refer to hidden processes within some postulated "ghost-in-the-machine", but rather are, dispositions which like running or jumping that can be demonstrated in and by the individual.

Socrates in *Menno*, contrives an argument purporting to demonstrate that the mind of man already possesses vast knowledge; suggesting that learning is not actually a process of learning anew, but rather a process of remembering. A thought or an idea that can simply be brought to one's recollection by engaging in intellectual discussion. A moment of recollection (to one's hypothetical 'inner man'). A moment that is not of significant importance, since the learner already supposedly had the information within himself.

It was Socrates who seems to have originated the conception of the 'soul'. That conception seems to have dominated European thinking ever since. For more than 2000 years it has been the standing assumption of civilized European man that he has a 'soul'. It remains an assertion and assumption. Nothing more.

It might be supposed that the individual is genetically endowed with a rudimentary capacity for a spontaneous rational process of the nature of simple <u>syllogism</u>. A major hypothesis, a minor hypothesis, and a conclusion (If A, and if B, then C.) In fact, I am inclined to suppose that all mammalian creatures have some native gift for at least the fundamentals of that capacity. A capacity that they utilize despite the fact that they have no formed concept of such. A concept that I recall having used long before I ever first even heard the word 'syllogism'. A part of our cultural everyday conversations and the daily currents of our life.

✳ ✳ ✳ ✳ ✳

Knowing

Those who were alive in Palestine in the first century AD were not better off than we in determining what to believe. For even "the contemporary of Jesus would have seen him only as a human being and was aware that God cannot be a human being." So we can see that "at any time, the problem of being a believer is the same. There is no evidence." Dogmatic assertions and controversial interpretations of histories. (p. 189 Popkin)

There is obviously a great deal of what is knowable to us mere mortals, of which we each own yet mostly but a great deal of ignorance. Why do we argue about what is knowable and of which we ourselves have come to know? Because even in these matters perhaps we are not all too sure that we do know it, since our perceptions of these are by no means unanimous. Or, we argue to enlighten these others and perhaps to our surprise, find ourselves too, having learned somewhat by dint of research, reflection, discussion, and argumentation. What we individually know of what are knowable things is limited indeed. Life is far too short and far too busy to permit of any mere mortal to make much more than a dent into the mountain of that which is theoretically knowable.

Why do we argue even more about that which is unknowable to we mere mortals? I am inclined to suppose that there is a vast such category.

R. G. Ingersol puts it thusly:
"Is there a God? I do not know.
Is man immortal? I do not know.
One thing I do know: that neither hope nor fear, belief nor denial, can change the (yet unknown) fact. It is as it is; and it will be as it must be.
We must wait. We may hope."
"And let us be cautious as to what we wish for."

Every believer in every religion is an atheist in the sense that though he courts his own Gods; he disbelieves in the gods of other religions. Nobody can be sure that what he believes is exactly correct. So one might aptly suggest that the most reasonable position lies in allowing first of an individual freedom of thought-and even freedom of speech.

A couple of broader notions of the deity:

— Pantheism-the world is God
— Panantheism-Not that the world is God, but that the world resides within His being.

Huxley's Metaphysical orientation of 4 ontological hypothesis:

1. There is no X
2. There is only one X. Materialism or Pantheism according as how you turn it...heads or tails.
3. There are two X's. Spirit and matter. = speculators
4. There are three X's. Gods, souls, matter = orthodox theologies.

X = underlying reality? or definitive explanation?

Huxley believed none are established factually, but #2 was the one he worked best with.

Can we explain what we perceive as having been created by an eternal God? But then we are left yet to explain the origin of the creator. To posit yet another Big Bang Theory-as it were. "Turtles, all the way down", as the English matron once put it. Infinite regression.

Most philosophers do not believe in God. Theologians do. Is there something within us that is beyond physical creation? An immortal "essence"? It is widely believed, and is the fundamental conception of most religions. Perhaps a comforting delusion if nothing else.

Has any man's reasoning ever gotten one to any definitive description or knowledge of God? Only dubious presumptions and tentative assertions. But none has seen God and we have but a cacophony of words and ideas about God that are widely proclaimed by those who claim to be in possession of The-Word-of-God and/or make claims of personal revelation from God. But if God were to stop you on the street, would you recognize his person-or that of Jesus? Would his any assertions of divinity (or our subjective assumption) be so obviously valid as to demand of you and I and the world our voluntary verdict of validity? There are and have been innumerable claims of personal 'revelations' from the Deity to one person or another throughout history. But even if any such claim were true, that 'revelation' would be nothing but 'hearsay' to you or I or anyone else, as Ethan Allen and Thomas Payne rightly remind us.

Shall we believe that God made himself known to Abraham? Why to Abraham, and not to me instead-or at least why not also to me? In fact, why not especially to me? It is not the case that I am just not listening; its just that I am not buying the sales pitch. Does God play favorites-as suggested by notions of predestination?

Though man is said by some to have been made in the image of God, God is then said to be everything that we are not (itself, but yet another assertion). Believers tend to conceive of God as a dynamic agent. But there is no tangible evidence to support this; nor hypothetical explanation of God that is irrefutable-and certainly not acceptable to the mass of mankind.

Shirmer (in Sc. Amer.) says "We can know nothing of God. Is God real or just a muddle? Made up? Or just a mystery? We can only say what he is not." Shall we struggle on through our lives with what we mere mortals can and do know? Or shall we abandon that, and then climb to the top of some geological pillar to lose ourselves in introspective eternal ponderings?

If God is real we should know more about him. Why would He be in hiding from we simpletons of the world? And if there is no certainty of the existence of God, then why complicate the business of deity with such notions as of Trinity? Just another Clinton-like rhetorical diversion to complicate issues.

All legitimate human knowledge arises from mankind's life experience in the natural world. From the senses, or from pondering, reflection, and dialectic-on the information provided by the senses, speculative philosophy, and science. No one believes that all of what is loosely called knowledge is absolutely valid. It need not be completely valid in order for one to find it useful to some purpose or another.

Either we are <u>not</u> free, and the Deity is responsible for what we call sin; or we are free, and responsible-but the Deity is then not all powerful. There is an ancient suggestion that one would not dare to look directly into the face of God (lest one hence would become blind-or something worse). One might suppose that to be a reality based upon some sort of empirical experience. More than one ancient religion has worshipped the sun as God. Some still do. To look directly into the sun for more than a few seconds would and does indeed result in blindness.

There seems a curious coincidence in the similarity of the words "sun" and "son". And another in the words "devil" and "evil".

"Supposing one becomes aware that there are two Gods who claim the same territory. A person might then suppose that only one could be valid, and that the other might have been invented by its priests. One might then postulate further that both might have been invented by priests." (as says Sagan in *The Dragons of Eden.*) Plurality of valid religions is contradictory to the theory of a single all powerful God.

There are and have been numbers of persons who claim themselves to possess personal deity. I have been acquainted with some in my employment at a Psychiatric hospital. Most of them certifiably insane. But, for obvious reasons, most of those wishing and attempting to establish themselves as religious leaders, would seem to see it as more prudent to pass themselves off as messenger, prophet, or descendent of God. Safer to play the role of spokesman and apologist for some god, rather than to be subject continuously to impossible requests and demands from 'the faithful' among the followers.

We readily suspect as foolish the 'sacred writings' of other people's beliefs as being dubious; and easily regard their persons as being gullible. That of the Hindu, the Mormon, the Islamist.... But as to our own hand-me-down words of wisdom, 'sacred books', cherished beliefs, and religious systems; we have been too long invested in them to permit of any much such similar suspicions. We are early and continuously admonished that any such suspicions are taboo. Forbidden, like the fruit of the tree of knowledge of good and evil, and wisdom.

> By education most have been misled;
> So they believe, because they were so bred.
> The priest continues what the nurse began,
> And thus the child imposes on the man.
> John Dryden

Perhaps you would be interested in what might be the details of my conclusions as to the nature of reality and whether or not there be a creator? As to that, I don't believe I'm in any immanent danger of coming soon to any definitive conclusion. I'm a slow thinker and student, and I have only had these 80-plus years to ponder the matter. One must be reminded of the common-place deception behind life's every day illusions and magical tricks: certainly comparable to the extreme difficulty of our getting free from deeply imbedded conceptual delusions.

✳ ✳ ✳ ✳ ✳

Levels Of Belief

Concerning especially politics but also with what ought to be straight forward news articles as well as financial advice we are inundated with supposedly well balanced announcements of 'information' and commentary from an assortment of TV-channels, radio stations, newspapers, and magazines. Diverse and politically slanted news so overburdened with Orwellian political correctness that we find it necessary always to try to read between the lines to guess at the reality of anything of what is being said. From all of this verbage, how would anyone come to grasp just what (if anything) is valid? There must be something from among this 'information' that is valid, but what? As for the statistics offered by the pundits on opposite sides of differing opinion, we come to be aware that 'figures lie, and that liars figure'. One can 'cherry pick' from an ample supply of available statistics to support almost any thesis.

What is apparent from much of the 'breaking news' is that it turns out eventually to have been erroneous and much opinionated. And so, 'the man on the street' pays mostly not a great deal of attention to the 'News'. Especially as he is preoccupied with the real and pertinent facts of every day life. In fact, when interviewed on the street, the responses of most of the citizenry indicate that the general public even among students on college campuses in not well informed even on American

History, or current events though they seem to have some acquired vague fixed opinions. And the behavior of mobs of college students on public beaches indicates an easy acceptance of lewd behavior and substance abuse.

✳   ✳   ✳   ✳   ✳

Erroneous Claims

<u>**Descartes**</u> launched his revolution in philosophy with "I think, therefore I am". Or, its obverse, that "I am, (have being) therefore I think". Each implies <u>that 'to be' (being) is to think</u>. Being, as distinguished from mere existence. ("If thought be life and strength and breath, and the want of thought be death..." Blake)

Thus did Descartes arrive at his certainty of consciousness; specifically, his individual self-consciousness. A natural implication of that is his further awareness or consciousness of his physical self and beyond that, a world filled with objects, persons, creatures, and things that are separate and distinct entities from himself. And yet, after bravely launching this revolution in philosophy, Descartes then retreats into a complex argument for the existence of God. "He retreats to the beliefs of the middle ages, even at the moment of launching a revolution that will abolish it." (Wm. Barrett). Perhaps he did so, in order to steer clear of difficulties with the all-powerful religious establishment of his era.

Those of us to whom it seems prudent to defer any fixed notions concerning God, or who specifically wish to stand outside of any particular belief in God... we needs must to search for other postulates to explain what we experience as the outside world.

From Essay on Man - by Pope
Know then thyself, presume not God to understand.
The proper study of mankind is man.
Placed on this isthmus of a middle state,

A being darkly wise, and rudely great.
With too much knoledge for the skeptic side.
With too much weakness for the stoic's pride.
He hangs between; in doubt to act or rest.
In doubt to deem himself a god or beast.
In doubt his mind or body to prefer.
Born but to die, and reasoning but to err,
Sole judge of truth, in endless error hurl'd.
The glory, the jest, and the riddle of the world.

If to be (being) is to think, then our sentient existence is intimately connected to thought. And analytical thought is intimately connected with what we call consciousness within the all encompassing 'mind' of man.

Our individual experience with the states of sleep, and the unconsciousness of severe injury, or of general anesthesia, would seem to suggest that our sense of being (existence) seems to shrink away into nothingness under those circumstances. In other words, that the sense-of-being, or existence, is a process dependent upon a wakeful and reasonably healthy cerebral activity. That without an ongoing cerebral function there is no [sense of] being, or existence. We would expect the same result with irreversible brain death.

What is generally referred to as **mind**, is not an object, an organ, a thing, an individual, or a separate being; but rather, **is a function of the brain or CNS** (f of CNS)-as is consciousness and self-consciousness.

In recent years much has been made of the "out-of-body-experience" of some who claim to have died. That is of the nature of psycho-babble, and has nothing to do with irreversible brain death-from which there is no evidence of resurrection among we mere mortals. "Near death experience" is probably what they are speaking of. Mistaken interpretations and bogus assertions founded upon admittedly uncommon experience in near-death situations. Due undoubtedly to what are only temporary CNS oxygen deprivations as is apt to occur for example in cardiac arrest, stroke, or massive blood loss. One's **claim** to have died **is not evidence** of having died. Evidence in fact that one has not died: and that attempt at resuscitation has been successful in these specific cases. (See, *Return from the Dead;* special program April 24, 2016; TV channel NGC 276; produced by Prof. Steven Laurey; at the University of Liege.) It is a special investigative program in quest of explanation into near-death experience and out-of-body experience)

These reports and allegations of near-death out-of-body experiences are not a vindication of the mind-body dualism of individual mortal man which is implicit misperception in the Philosophy of Descartes, And misperceptions certainly are not uncommon to we mere mortals even when fully conscious and in good health.

✳   ✳   ✳   ✳   ✳

Authoritative Assertions

<u>DOGMA</u> is religious doctrine asserted and proclaimed on the basis of alleged personal revelation and/or allegedly authoritative scripture, or ancient traditional belief. It need not be erroneous, but is by no means commonly synonymous with truth. It is simply a <u>fervently promoted interpretation of reality based upon limited available information and facts</u>. Assertions often to bolster a particular self-serving agenda or religious system. Not infrequently based upon even willfully errant belief. When new facts are presented, scientific authorities take pains to verify before accepting the changes as a matter or course; while religious dogma desperately resists the necessity of change. We are particularly concerned with the attitudes and teachings of various religions which pay little heed to new discovery nor heed illuminating new information. Religions still uphold much of their incongruous dogma that dates from ancient and medieval times. As H.G. Wells opined in the early 1900's, that "the religious life of western nations is going on in a house of history built upon sand."

Part of the problem we have with Philosophy, undoubtedly has to do with our approach to the subject. We run into a stone mountain of obstruction on our thought trail, and spend a week bumping our head against it, yet, accomplishing no intellectual work (for there has been no progress). In the physical world, we can move actual mountains by blasting them into fragments, and carting them away piecemeal. Perhaps philosophical roadblocks might one day, be handled analogously? Yet, our methods for doing so seem generally still not yet conceived of, nor yet effective despite the intellectual thought, efforts, and intentions of a host of philosophical personage down through the ages-the likes of Aquinas, Descartes, and Spinoza. No wonder then, that the <u>labor of mental effort</u> (thought) is often regarded condescendingly compared to the mechanical physical labors of the body. This, even though the reality is that 20 or 25 percent of the energy we use each day is consumed in the CNS. Nor is there an easy method for an observer to watch with reassurance, or measure the any progress of the labor of mental effort-presuming even that a given philosopher is concerting his efforts upon philosophy, rather than simply dozing or daydreaming behind the pretense of that effort.

"Our most advanced thinking can be effectively and reliably evaluated only on paper. The thought we set down in writing, thereby reveals defects that would otherwise escape correction." (p. 305 from *Out of Chaos*)

My personal experience with Philosophy to date, leaves me with some rather <u>particular impressions</u> concerning that subject. As it seems to me:

- Philosophy aims at the general, specifically. From which position it has hopes of progressing to specifics, as they arise. (Deductive reason).
- Philosophy might also deal painstakingly with the particular by way of example and then gradually work towards a goal of valid generalities. (Inductive reason).

- Philosophy ought best strive toward objectivity.
- Philosophy must deal extensively with the field of psychology.
- All things and all processes call upon us to recognize them and proceed to their truths (or at least they allow this).
- The data upon which philosophy can work is various, and with various degrees of reliability. The data with which it deals include the following:
    a) sense data.
    b) personal and logical analysis of that data.
    c) pondering reflections of past experience.
    d) tentative conclusions and the further analysis thereof.
    e) mystical insights?
    f) personal experience and experimentation.
    g) the ideas and opinions of others-writings
    h) the behavior of others.
    i) the self-analysis of one's own behavior.
    j) direct communication with others.

- One must always question one's own motives, ideas, conclusions, and even one's own sincerity.
- Nevertheless, one must 'trust thyself' first.
- Listen to others and discuss their ideas with them, but concerning what they may say about what they believe, put more confidence in what you can see of their deportment, actions, and behavior.
- Be ready to believe that others too, (even the great and those entrusted with 'authority' may err in their own understanding of themselves; and the complexities of reality.
- Make reasoning your starting point and main tool.
- Distrust emotions enough to regularly scrutinize them in the light of reason.

From *"A Studied Impression of That Which Is"*

The dogma of the-ghost-in-the-machine would maintain that there exist two separate entities; bodies and 'minds'. And that they exist as separate components of each individual-separate entities. Would then go on to maintain that there are mechanical causes of bodily movements; <u>and also</u> mental causes of bodily movements.

Thus it can thus be said that each human being does have a mind. And that each has a body. Mind and body however are not two separate constituents. They are but two separate aspects the one entity-a human being. Just as in like manner a lone silver dollar has both a 'heads' and a 'tails' as two aspects of its existence as a single coin.

Consciousness is an attribute of the mind. One of which you and I have personal evidence in our daily lives since perhaps rather early in our lives. It having been so long with us, it is difficult to say when we first paid it much heed. Perhaps when in the course of our education when we first encountered a name for it did we first begin to recognize it as being more or less preeminent in our lives. Perhaps recognized earliest as mere wakefulness. Though it has been said by some to be the earliest and most obvious of things which we know about ourselves, I am inclined to take some little issue with this. From the recollections of my own past, I rather believe that in my childhood and youth, I was primarily aware of my own physical body. It was only somewhere in my adult years, and only when my attention was called to the fact that I was enticed conceptually to acknowledge to myself the awareness of my conscious awareness. And even then, I have continued to acknowledge my physicality as equally fundamental to my existence.

One in childhood gradually learns the physical limits of his extension in time and space to be located at the outer perimeter of his finger-tips, as it were. And I note the boundaries and limits of my physical being even as I more vaguely note the limits of my intangible political-social influence within civil society.

"Body and 'mind' would appear to be connected in some manner which is difficult to conceive." But are they not but two aspects of one being, as suggested by Spinoza? A monad then, rather than a Cartesian duality? The conscious and the subconscious mind seem both to produce effects on the body, just as the condition of the body is decidedly able to affect the 'mind'. I.e. as a state of delirium in severe illness disorders the conscious 'mind'. Or as in sleep the disorderly state of the subconscious runs amok without corrective influence from either the internal rational 'mind', or without a connection to the <u>veracity and reference point of the real external world</u> (<u>the moral value of reality</u>). In my waking state, I often recall and ponder my dreams. Strange, are the discontinuity and oddities of those dreams. But in my dreams, I never reference back to states of wakefulness to ponder their meaning. I have though, on one occasion pondered one dream in which was embedded another dream.

The notion that the physical substance of my CNS (neurons) is a separate entity from a non-tangible essence of my 'mind' poses even this considerably additional difficulty. <u>If</u> intangible 'mind' and the cellular tissues of the brain were <u>not</u> merely two aspects of the same CNS (one the tangible neuronal substance; and the other, the <u>function</u> of that substance), then what third inexplicable something could one postulate as the connection and point of contact between tangible neurons and intangible 'mind'?

Humanity

Life Cycle

Speaking of animal life-forms that reproduce sexually, one might say that all come into existence with some native inherited sense of awareness, and basic reflexes, and intuition such as to endow each individual with some statistical possibility of survival from inception into growth, maturation, and reproductive adult status through what one might call a "life cycle". A cycle which includes the death and demise of the individual. That is to say, predispositions, basic reflexes, and instincts that are provided to the individual from instructions (information) carried in the chromosomal DNA and which is passed subsequently from one generation to the next, in perpetuity.

Of animalcular life forms it appears that their lives are guided (from highest to lowest life forms) by:

- Life Mandate + Reflex + Instinct + Amygdala (emotion) + Inhibition + Frontal Lobe CEO + Mind.
- Life Mandate + Reflex + Instinct + Amygdala + Inhibition + Frontal Lobe CEO.
- Life Mandate + Reflex + Instinct + Amygdala + Inhibition.
- Life Mandate + Reflex + Instinct + Amygdala.
- Life Mandate + Reflex + Instinct.
- Life Mandate + Reflex.

Beyond all of that, our own species-Homo sapiens-is considered by ourselves to be the most advanced form of life here on planet Earth. Our genetic endowments include such features as legs for transportation, arms and hands for tool making, defense, and locomotion, five sensory modes with which to bring us a steady stream of information from the world (of which we are a part), vocal cords to give us the potential for speech and language, and a CNS with conscious awareness and native intelligence that enables us to elude much of the hazard of this world and to shape our environment to better serve our needs and aesthetic comforts of life.

Instinct

Like reflexes, instinct may be said to be our unlearned responses which can be supposed to be inherited with the DNA which passes down to each subsequent generation. The tendencies to walk and run, to eat and play, to fight and to escape. To woo and to wed and to love our children. Useful economies of behavior developed in a species to meet those recurrent exigencies in the career of the race. To meet exigencies without the delay of fatal deliberation. Useful and necessary, for often in extremes, there is no time for thought.

But by instinct we at times go awry. We do not fear the carriers of deadly malaria or yellow fever. Yet, we do fear thunder and the dark which themselves are not a significant threat. We suffer more from public scorn than from our own idleness, ignorance, and folly.

Yes, ever since the origin of civilization, instinct has been at times useful, but in some situations is so inadequate that human life has also found a demand for the exercise of a capacity for reason. A potential which is also inherited into us. Instincts predispose and reason oft must overcome. And so though cautious of instinct, we learn to use and manage it-but carefully. Man is fearful of the wild beast but learns with caution to hunt and even to face his predators in self-defense.

✳   ✳   ✳   ✳   ✳

Reason

Along with Ethan Allen, I too conceive or Reason as being man's one true oracle. That oracle is there to be consulted in the face of uncertainties and dilemma. Reflex, instinct, and acquired habit equip a person with mechanism for rapid response as we confront the situations and obstacles of the day-by-day of our daily lives. Useful in their impulsive immediateness to situations with which we are regularly confronted and which require prompt response-where delay in response can readily be fatal. No time in such situations for the exercise of one's time consuming rational judgment where that delay can prove fatal.

But much of that with which we are confronted and to which we must respond is not of any immediacy, and gives cause and time for the exercise of reason to provide one with the sound opinion and judgment that are better suited to one's long term goals and one's philosophy of life where one can tease out the details of dilemma and uncertainty. Even so, as Ben Franklin cautions, it is of the utmost importance the our opinion are in close alignment with reality.

This life's journey is one of largely unforeseen consequences. "What man is, can best be understood in terms of how he came to be what he now is, and what he can make of himself in time to come." (Abel p. xxi) Logic and our experience of life informs us that mankind is but a part of the universe. It is not reasonable to expect that the part should ever understand the whole. A little modesty and a little honesty are enough to make us aware that life and the world are too complex and subtle for our imprisoned and constrained individual minds. It has been said that "Life might be seen as the art of drawing sufficient conclusions from insufficient premises."

✳   ✳   ✳   ✳   ✳

Primitive Infant

Though helpless and demanding, the primitive currents of the infant 'mind' are totally of the nature of what we would now call 'Id'. Devoid of any mental process of rational Ego, let alone of idealistic notions of 'Superego'. We humans, possess a brain instinctively avid to learn and destined gradually to become ever more able to fend for ourselves. Meanwhile, there is a necessary reciprocity between the infant's caregiver (mother and family) and child that must progress to some degree of civilizing process being enforced upon the child over a period of years. "Yes" and "no" needs must become an early part of the child's understanding. The reasoning of ego and superego only gradually becomes a part of the child's mental and learning process. As matters progress the infant comes to understand that he must begin to exercise some self-restraint and self-discipline as part of the dialectical contract with mother, family, and society at large. Elements of Ego-as it were. In consequence of the child's physical dependency and that civilizing process, the child becomes psychologically attached to the caregiver family and comes to experience anxiety from any much separation.

By degree, the external disciplinary control to the infant and child is to some greater or lesser degree absorbed and internalized into what we may speak of as a maturing 'mind'. Id, Ego, and Superego come to some equilibrium of proportion within the psyche, to where the 'mind' becomes ever more self-disciplined with increasing stores of informed recollections, memory, knowledge, and experience.
[I continue to use the term 'mind' throughout the entirety of this book. But I use it with the clear implication and understanding that the 'mind' is but a function of the brain or CNS-not a separate entity from the brain. And that the word 'mind', is not to be considered as interchangeable with words such as 'soul', or 'spirit', for example. Words that are overly ripe with troublesome connotations.]

In our infancy and childhood, we conceive ourselves primarily as physical beings. The underlying barbarian "Heavy Bear" remains within, but the child's rampaging Id impulses are modified and abated by counterbalancing forces of self-control.

＊　＊　＊　＊　＊

The Heavy Bear (Id?)
The heavy bear who goes with me,
. . . .
That heavy bear that sleeps with me.
Howls in his sleep for a world of sugar,
. . . .
That inescapable animal walks with me,
Has followed me since the black womb held,
. . . .
Dragging me with him in his mouthing care,
Amid the hundred million of his kind,
the scrimmage of appetite everywhere.
　　　　　　by Delmore Schwartz

＊　＊　＊　＊　＊

Roots Of Civil Decency

The evolving conceptualizing mind comes to differentiate within itself some incompatible predispositions. Such terms as Id, Ego, and Superego mind, consciousness, subconscious, soul, spirit, and a multitude of the concepts of our culture are synthesized in our languages as pragmatic conceptual devices. Words intended to facilitate our perceptive grasp and communication about and among ourselves concerning the nature of our intangible realities. Realities with which we must deal as we bumble about in the darkness of our hopefully ever-lessening ignorance of ourselves and of a world and universe which is quite beyond the poor powers of our individual comprehension in so limited a time as is available to each of we mere mortals.

The coined words of our analytic conception then represent the components of one's conscious and subconscious mind with which we can probe and ponder the ambiguities and ambivalence within the mind.

As **Huxley** puts it, "each one of us is potentially mind-at-large. But insofar as we are animals, our business is at all costs to survive. To make biological survival possible, mind-at-large has to be funneled through the reducing valve of the brain and nervous system. What comes out at the other end is a measly trickle of the kind of consciousness which will help us to stay alive". To formulate and express even this reduced awareness, man has invented those symbolic systems of communication which we call languages. Every individual is both the beneficiary and victim of the linguistic tradition into which he has been born. Beneficiary, in as much as the language gives him access to the accumulate records of other people's experience (and knowledge); the victim, in so far as it confirms him in the belief that reduced awareness is the only awareness and as it bedevils his sense of reality so that he is all to apt to take his (personal) concepts for 'data' and conceive that his words necessarily represent actual things. That which, in the language of religion, is called 'the world', is the universe of reduced awareness-expressed, and as it were, petrified by language. [see Huxley]

Contest with those about us, upon whom we are dependent, becomes manifest as objectives and motives clash in the complexities of our daily lives. The necessity of compromise is enforced upon the infant mind. The infant psyche has thus encountered the ever present internal war within the self. A war that manifests itself in consciousness as confusion, stirred emotion, uncertainty, and dilemma. Id, especially is at odds with slowly evolving Superego. Much of what we designate as Ego is rational and is useful to the adult in contest with the world and his milieu as he struggles to compete and barter his course through life in the unforgiving world. At times when Ego overplays its hand, the rational impulse is swayed toward the pseudo-rational which we call 'rationalizing'. A defense of that within which is more of the nature of purely ungenerous self-serving Id.

Infant is immersed in immense variability of tangible things, processes, and scenarios. And becomes acquainted with ideas and concepts that influence an external universe far beyond one's available time and ability to perceive in fullness. And it is beyond an infant's immediate ability to enquire into any significant fraction thereof, though flooded continuously with sensory input to the CNS. Input which arrives as a chaotic tide that far outpaces the infant's limited ability to perceptively organize its fullness into one's understanding. What one might grasp on one's own is necessarily much limited.

But language exists among all tribes and races of mankind and is acquired within two or three years by the infant within the family. Once gradually acquired, it greatly facilitates the child's depth and grasp of what we each may learn. A grasp which is much enhanced by that ability of we mere mortals to exchange and preserve information among ourselves in speech and in written word.

Much, for example, of what we visually perceive would pass into-and out of-our awareness except that we gain instruction from those about us to point things out to us and facilitate our speed of comprehension. Language can be said to be the key to our mortal liberation from a mere sensory world. (see Higbrow)

I am led to suppose that in the process of evolving into personhood and self-awareness, one first begins to conceive of himself primarily as a physical being. And that only eventually does one begin to differentiate himself as an entity separate from his mother and those of his family and close milieu. One comes then to acquire 'personality' (differentiating skills, propensities, habits and character traits) and gradually generates (and becomes ever more aware of) his evolving private thoughts, ideas, and concepts.

And the intangible evolving cognitive mind of infancy ('f of CNS') is simultaneously to become aware of the possession of its own tangible physical being, which is situated within both a local and a universal world. A world and universe which is ambiguous as to cause, purpose, and relevance to the individual. And one comes to terms with his own separate individual physical being and its demands upon one's own mental processes and efforts. Increasingly aware of the harsh, and unforgiving outer world of which one is a part. But from which he possesses a small separate individual being. A confusing world which makes but little free concession to one's whims, wishes, and hopes.

"It is largely in one's milieu of relationships with one another that we find meaning." (p. 66 Highbrow) Consequently we find utility in nurturing such concepts as caring, fairness, respect, loyalty, and impurity. (Ibid p. 64)

But yet one is primarily preoccupied in his self-concepts and in his being as a physical entity-as he comes into his adult maturity and gradually becomes a self-sufficient and self-supporting person. Continues thusly into the rutting season of life and gradually finds himself ever more saddled with 'responsibility' and a host of other forms of constraint and guiding expectations from within and without. Finding oneself eventually required ever more to deal with those about him conceptually and socially, one begins ever more to be dealing with the intangibles of his evolving realities of life [social, political and philosophical entanglements].

Eventually one's mortal frame and physical strength begins to wane and one becomes progressively ever more aware of his own mortality. And as a life proceeds into the sunset years, there seems to be a certain tendency for one to regard the self more as, of-the-nature-of 'mind'. Mind being **a** function of CNS, which imparts to one a conscious awareness of ourselves and our surroundings and situation. And one comes to regard oneself ever less much as of a physical entity; and ever somewhat more of a conceptual mind.

And from that altered perspective, one can look back and more clearly acknowledge that that intangible something (mind) has been a significant component of one's being for lo these many decades of one's mortal existence.

We human beings are endowed with **consciousness**-the awareness of one's own being. A consciousness that extends to the awareness of one's surroundings and ever-changing situation in the dangerous and complex world of one's existence. Though we each possess this inscrutable self-perception in our solitary self-conscious mind ('f of CNS'), the business of our lives in the extant world of reality is lived in the context of relationships with other things, individual beings, and communications with other minds. A matter of reciprocity and communication through spoken and written language, and the perceptive (intuitive?) reading of the responses and behaviors of other persons, beings, and creatures. We learn and teach one another about life through that reciprocity with other beings. Each contributing his personal insight. Each insight which when combined with other variant insights has potential to broaden one's perceptions into something of the nature of an 'in-depth' and more informed understanding of the any matter under consideration. A sort of synoptic view of larger conception to our understandings. (p. 147 Bateson) A meeting of the minds, as it were.

Yet, even in the exercise of wisdom, we are confronted forever with dilemma. What is enough? What is too much? What is reasonable? What is profitable? And what is possible? What is knowable in our times? What is potentially knowable? What is unknowable to we mere mortals.

"The letter that you do not write, the apology that you do not offer, the food that you do not put out for the cat-all these can be sufficient and effective messages; because zero (in context) can be meaningful. And it is the recipient of the message who creates the context. This power to context is the recipient's skill-to acquire which is his half of the co-evolution" [of a dialectic]. (p. 51 Bateson)

A human being's central nervous system (CNS) is the substrate for human consciousness and intelligence. The CNS of man is considered to be the most intricately evolved and endowed among all living creatures and consequently possesses the greatest capacity for intelligence and intellectual endeavor. That endeavor being the pursuit of information, knowledge, and truth; or the application of those capacities to the solution of life's problems. It goes without saying, that the solution to one problem can often make one aware of, or be the cause of yet another problem. A matter that is especially obvious to us in the malfunctioning of government. Hence, the ultimate and most elusive quest of mankind is for an intelligence that is crowned by wisdom-knowledge, information, perception and truth enough to foresee the consequences of our action. And ever cautious in its legislation and judgments.

We acquire our knowledge and information through time and by experience one split-second at a time. In order for that information to be useful into our immediate and distant future (as does occur) it would seem obvious that we each possess what we shall call <u>memory</u>. Some ongoing access to an awareness of things of our individual immediate and remote past. An indispensable memory which we recognize to be of rather limited capacity and which not infrequently proves to be somewhat inaccurate. A memory which we must finally conclude to be somewhat malleable. A memory which can be expanded, fortified, and prolonged with mnemonic exercises. Prolonged with repetition, when coated with emotion, fitted with poetic verse, by attachment to melody, aided by the written word, or supported by use of electronic storage devices.

On Consciousness

Solipsism

Conscious awareness would appear to be an inner subjective state and a private individual possession. Solipsism as a <u>Theory of Mind</u> is speculative, and concludes that one can't be sure that other minds exist. Solipsism-unable to discover any logically satisfactory evidence warranting one person in believing that there exist minds other than his own. Able to witness what the body of another persons does, but claiming to be unable to witness what that person's mind does.

I note that I have a definite animal certainty of the existence of an outer world beyond the boundaries of my personal embodied being, and my own physical body in its interactions with the world and its inhabitants. But just as certain to me is the matter of my own self-conscious awareness. I conceive I have at least a degree of transparency to myself (i.e. one's conscious awareness). But though I have a certainty of the animal existence of other persons, yet I have only limited and occasional evidence such as to suggest a self-consciousness within anyone other than myself. Namely, those with whom I have had at least occasional extended conversations and interactions. Mainly relatives and a few friends. But still, enough evidence from my interactions with others to presume its presence in perhaps all of mankind.

It is my inclination then to abandon Solipsism. For one's notion of one's own 'mind' would seem to have no basis for existence without the existence of other 'minds'. Somewhere in the early years of life, a child seems ordinarily to come to the conclusion that those about him must have 'minds', for the child begins to be able to guess what the other is about to do; and begins to perceive that they can likewise often guess what he himself is 'up to'.

And thus it can be said that we discover and regularly interact with the minds of family, friends, and those with whom we mingle. We interact with them physically in sports and athletic contest, and less directly as fellow classmates through our years of schooling. From among those many, we become especially close to some select few, whom we come to regard as personal friends and with whom we pal around in our leisure hours. We mutually select one another largely on the basis of our mental compatibilities. A meeting of the minds, as it were. We are obviously aware of the reality of their physical bodies, but we don't scrutinize their bodies closely; and we tend to be widely accepting of the parameters of that. What is more important, is that we come to recognize within one another the intangible qualities of that which constitutes the minds of one another. Their character and quality of intellect which we can observe in their customs, deportment, and habits. And we recognize their intellectual interests which we discover to bear a compatible affinity to our own.

Through the years we study and read widely and come to honor and respect the qualities of mind of persons we have never met nor even see. Persons even of older generations and times. We commune as it were, with minds which they have exposed in their written words.

We do much of our learning by the conditioning of drill. A form of learning which largely dispenses with the need for a terribly high intelligence. Training on the other hand is an aid to the improvement of intelligence. The ability to learn by rote is also a facet which gives some evidence of intelligence. And there certainly seems to be considerable utility in the application of rote memory even in persons of high intelligence (i.e. the alphabet, number sequence, multiplication tablets, etc.), but this capacity is limited. So that, in general, it is more economical of energy to learn rules, and to practice at applying them.

✳   ✳   ✳   ✳   ✳

Consciousness

Consciousness implies memory as well as self-awareness. Though I have a conscious awareness of myself in most of my hours of wakefulness, it seems not so when I am asleep. And at times I am very much more aware of myself, as when I am embarrassed in the presence of others. As when I am unwillingly become the momentary center of unwanted attention.

"Man's self-concept is not a single concept, but a cluster of images and abstract perspectives on his various (real and imaginary) traits and characteristics, the sum total of which can never be held in focal awareness at any one time. That sum is experienced, but it is not perceived as such."

"The Visibility principle" suggests that man desires and needs the experience of (psychological) self-awareness that results from perceiving himself as an objective existence." And he is able to achieve that experience through interaction with the consciousness of other living entities. (N. Brandon)

One's consciousness needs a sense of self. It hardly seems likely it could exist apart from one's physical being. There is something about consciousness that <u>is</u> delusional-pure supposition. That something is this: that one's consciousness exists beyond time and space. It does not. A comforting delusion, perhaps. But of mythical conception and widely propagated by various theologies and religions. The reality is that when the brain ceases to function efficiently, consciousness is diminished and is eventually extinguished when confronted with massive die-off of cells of the cerebral cortex.

Consciousness is primary both to our organic and our intangible conceptual existence. It too, being a component of 'mind'. It is <u>a function</u> of the neural activity of the cerebral cortex.

Most people when queried would seem to have the impression that the essence of what constitutes their being resides at some particular location in their physical body. Perhaps it is where we perceive that our thinking takes place, or perhaps where we sense our emotional being to be centered. At times perhaps from where we experience physical pleasure. Commonly therefore persons will designate the anterior chest wall, beneath which lies the heart. Certainly throughout one's life a person becomes aware of the change of pace and increased pounding of the heart beat in response to sudden change in one's emotional status. More persons, however, will commonly point to their head, where they perceive that thinking takes place. (p. 70 Marris) And when confused, in a state of pondering, or puzzlement, many people will scratch their forehead, as though to suggest that some activity is occurring at that area.

I first had cause to consider the matter while in college and in Medical School. At least since that time, I tend to regard that the locus of that hypothetical 'inner man' would 'seem to be' directly behind and between my eyes. As though perhaps seated right in the anatomical sella tursica (the Turkish saddle) in which is actually situated the pituitary gland. I still semi-perceive it that way, although I do not actually believe it to be so. But I do believe that what goes on in my head ('**f** of CNS') is more of the essence of what and who I am than is this aging carcass which is diminishingly yet under my command. And yet, neither can I abandon my believe that my enlivened body remains a part of the essence of who I am. A seemingly natural tendency to stumble into such cognitive dissonance. Or at least an acknowledgment of the reality of one's uncertainty.

The (conscious) mind (*f* of CNS) contains no things; no cats or dogs or people. No cars or houses, nor toys, guns, or bombs. It contains ideas, concepts, and information about things and how those things function. It contains no time or space; only ideas about time and space (Bateson p.146).

✳   ✳   ✳   ✳   ✳

Degree Of Consciousness

Perhaps Homo sapiens might be thought of as an important part of nature's mechanism of being aware of itself? For we are widely inquisitive about the universe as well as the dangers and of the multitude of creatures of the world in which we abide.

Animals of species other than ourselves would appear to have nothing more than a here-and-now limited consciousness connected to some limited rudimentary (largely unorganized) memory. They many (like ourselves) have a herd consciousness-a universal consciousness among those of its own kind; and an awareness of a great many other strange creatures of other species all about them which are not a part of their herd. Many of which are a danger and a threat to themselves and their own clustered herd to which they instinctively cling for protection and direction.

One must perhaps consider that wakefulness alone is not conscious awareness. [Recall the Terry Schibo controversy of some years past] Some level of <u>focus of attention</u> (intent and effort) would needs must be added to mere wakefulness alone. And the evidence of that focused attention to make itself manifest in some sort of activity-i.e. to raise and exercise an arm, to get up and look for an item, to pick up and scan a book, to write a note, to make a phone call, or at least make an effort to feed oneself etc. The driving dynamic behind purpose and intent we may well suppose to be located somewhere in the neural networks that include the prefrontal cortex area of the brain. Focus of the senses upon an object or purpose though a native potential of the infant, is to be acquired to its fullest degree only by long practice and experience as is its native potential for the coordinated use of its arms and legs.

Infants startle and thrash their limbs about to no purpose or effect for months before they gradually begin to use the limbs to some seemingly intended purpose. Only after many months can they begin to take a few tentative and clumsy steps; and develop coordination enough of their arms and hands to begin clumsily to feed themselves. The tasks they perform improve with repetition and determined practice.

❋ ❋ ❋ ❋ ❋

Attending

It seems prudent in the name of clarity to distinguish between superficial <u>perception, versus the attending or focusing</u> of one's limited consciousness. "Visual perception is not entirely a mechanical recording of sensory elements, but a creative grasp of reality." We perceive the night sky, but do we attend to it as a whole? No. Too vast for mere mortal capacity. As one does with a telescope, one can attend to only one small spec of light in the entire night sky in any given instant. And though one can cast the sensitivity of one's entire retina upon say 180 degrees of the sky at any one instant, yet, the central fovea with which one 'attends' is but a minuscule part of that. The remainder needs must exist in a vastly more vague concept of one's perceptions. Dim perceptions, one might say. While one's tiny island of actual awareness is as though centered on a single word or phrase of a single page of a thick tomb on a vast subject. Which is compatible with the fact that visual acuity of the fovea is 20/20 while diminishing to a mere 20/400 immediately beyond the fovea centralis.

Mere sensory perception is largely a passive reception. An intentional focused perception is an active inquiry. "It is a task to be accomplished." (p. 41 Abel) Neither in physics nor in human affairs is there a determinate, ordered reality which can be known by the passive reception of discrete sense impressions. (p. 116 Abel)

To repeat, thought is the focused intellectual endeavor of a consciousness in the pursuit of knowledge or truth OR the application of that knowledge or truth to the solution of problems. Ever in quest of the useful theory and certainties which are "the wages of mental work, not gifts of revelation." (p. 238 Ryle)— Building a theory is likened to traveling: having a theory is likened to being at a destination. The difference between truth and knowledge is that "<u>knowledge</u> must be justified by evidence or good reasons." (p. 78 of Abel)

Truth seems more of just a general category of philosophy which can be somewhat refined and more specific by the addition of valid knowledge and demonstrable validity.

One's consciousness includes an ability to focus and point the senses and mental powers inquiringly and creatively. "The consciousness that you and I perceive is constructed from the avalanche of sensations that pour into the wakened brain" [from the external world, as well as from our own internal sensory-motor system]. "Working at a furious pace, the brain summons up its memories to screen and make sense of the incoming chaos. Only a small part of that information of perception is selected for higher-order processing. From that small part, small segments are enlisted through symbolic imagery to create the white-hot core of activity which we call the conscious mind." (p. 132 Wilson)

Consciousness (of one's 'rational intangible mind') is the most obvious and real thing that we of our 'Homo sapiens' species possess. So says Nicholas Humphrey, and I grasp at least a partial reality in that. Consciousness is with us in the waking state even often when one is immersed in the black of darkest night. [But still, I am tempted to suspect that to be more true as one matures and ages.] It is not an illusion and not a paranormal phenomenon. Conscious awareness is an intangible product or function of the brain. Each individual 'mind', comes into being as a function of one's brain. An intangible function that deals with the perceptions of the physical realities of one's world and the interactions of one's physical reality in that external physical world and universe.

❋   ❋   ❋   ❋   ❋

We seem as though to dwell at once in two separate universes-the real world, and the conceptual world. The cognitive, rational mind is a function of one's physical CNS and being, but which contemplates and deals also with such intangibilities as ideas, beliefs, concepts, possibilities, probabilities, hopes, and plans-all of which are relevant to one's passage through and from this mortal coil. That "'mind' is an aggregate of interrelated parts or components" of the CNS. "Mental processes are always a sequence of interactions between those parts". (pp. 102-103 Bateson) We are conscious of the products of the mind's perceptions, even though unconscious of the greater part of the process. (p. 97 Bateson)

✳   ✳   ✳   ✳   ✳

Self Knowledge

Consciousness implies memory as well as self-awareness. It has previously been held that the alert and wakeful mind cannot help being aware of all the supposed occupants of its 'private stage'. And that it can also deliberately scrutinize, by a species of non-sensuous perception, at least some of its own states and operations. This constant awareness is an aspect of <u>consciousness</u>. There is said to be another non-sensuous inner perception called <u>introspection</u> which has been thought to provide one with self-knowledge.

This introspection has been supposed to be exempt from error by virtue of the two-fold privileged access to its own doings (consciousness and introspection). An insight which was said to make its self-knowledge superior in quality, as well as prior in genesis to its grasp of other things. A problem with this suggestion is that the content of one's <u>sub-consciousness</u> seems to be more vast than that of one's consciousness. And that the subconscious is now thought to be mostly impervious to the supposed probing of the introspection process.

It is as though to suggest that one may doubt the evidence of one's five senses, but not doubt the deliverances to consciousness of introspection.

It is said on the other hand, that though one can thus have certainty of one's own states and operations, yet one cannot have any such access to the minds of others. This long held dogma has taken so strong a hold on the thought of philosophers, psychologists, and many laymen that it is now thought to be enough to say (on behalf of the dogma of the mind as a postulated second theatre,) that its consciousness from introspection discovers some sort of scenes enacted upon some sort of private inner stage.

What we call introspection is supposedly a species of internal perception, but one which is probably more of the nature of retrospection, especially if connected to some one of the many inner agitations to which we mere mortals are so commonly predisposed.

The Cartesian dogma of the-ghost-in-the-machine tends to argue that the imputed objects of consciousness and introspection cannot be myths, since we are conscious of them and can introspectively observe them. But Riley argues that consciousness and introspection cannot be what they are officially described as being, since their supposed objects (mind and 'an inner man') have only a conceptual existence from the realm of Ideas.

Riley sets out to prove that this self-knowledge is not attained by consciousness or introspection. He indicates that knowledge of what there is to be known about (this 'essence' of) other people is restored to approximate parity with self-knowledge. For he points our that the things that one can find out about oneself are the same as the sorts of thing that one can find out about other people. And that the methods of discovering them are much the same. A residual difference in the subconscious supplies of the requisite data makes some differences in degree between what I can know about myself and what I can know about you, but these differences are not all in favor of self-knowledge.

In fact, however, we do discover the mind, consciousness, and motives of other people. A process that is not wholly immune from possibility of error. We do this by examining their history-the way a person reacts now and has reacted on previous occasions in similar situations.

"The way in which a person discovers his own long-term motives is the same as the way in which he discovers those of others"-by recalling his own history of reactions and behavior. And he can perform thought experiments of fancying himself confronted by tasks and opportunities which have not actually occurred. (p. 90 Riley)

In general, "we think that <u>an impartial and discerning spectator is a</u> <u>better judge</u> of a person's prevailing character and motives, as well as of his habits, abilities, and weaknesses, than is that person himself." (ibid p. 90)

This "view is directly contrary to the theory which holds that an agent possesses a privileged access to the so-called springs of his own actions and is, because of that access, able and bound to discover, (without inference or research) from what motives he tends to act and from what motive he acted on any particular occasion." (ibid pp. 90-91)

❋   ❋   ❋   ❋   ❋

Seat Of Consciousness

To what part of the CNS might consciousness be most closely associated? Seemingly vital to that process are the frontal lobes and their interconnection to the limbic system-where the functions of emotion and the site of acquisition of memory seem to be located. And yet, the midbrain "reticular formation" seems also to be a vital component to that which we call consciousness. A lesser quality of conscious perhaps. such as is probably possessed by creatures further on down the phylogenic tree i.e. reptiles and amphibians. The reticular formation is said to function as an off/on switch to the process of <u>a higher level of consciousness in our species-as compared</u> <u>to other mammals</u>. And much higher as compared to amphibians and reptiles. Researchers note that information once acquired through the five senses is made available from the various cortical areas as a working memory in the dorsal frontal lobe of the CNS, as suggested by PET scan studies of blood flow in the brain. It would seem to be within the interactive relationship between the limbic system and the frontal lobes where human consciousness is experienced. It is into our frontal lobes that one retrieves, ponders, and weighs its store of information before deciding to initiate or withhold a contemplation or bodily act, or behavior.

The <u>limbic system</u> is located centrally at the base of the cerebral cortex, and includes the amygdala, the hippocampus, the hypothalamus, the olfactory bulbs, the pituitary, and the thalamus (which is located in the uppermost part of the midbrain). A group of interconnected loci that are <u>broadly concerned with emotions and memory</u>.

One must suppose consciousness to be considered as a major characteristic of the intangible 'mind'. If, supposing that this intangible 'mind' and the tangible CNS were separate entities; then arises the enigma as to what part of the CNS is the intangible mind and consciousness in vital linkage? And what could possibly be the nature of that linkage?? Something tangible or something intangible? You can see of course that this is unworkable. (p. 200 Abel)

❋   ❋   ❋   ❋   ❋

Forms Of Consciousness
from *THE QUANTUM ATAVIST* - Dr Amit Goswami
(A challenge to traditional views of existence and reality.) -Abstract by RGB-

The background of existential reality is created by consciousness acting upon the probabilities and possibilities of Quantum Physics. One might postulate more than one **form of consciousness**. The <u>first</u> being <u>local consciousness</u> within the 'mind' of each human being. We each create our own reality by thought, which commonly influences or leads to action-to thus arrive at the goals and objectives and the ultimate accomplishments of our being. A <u>second</u> **form of consciousness** being the shared consciousness of the family and the tribe. A <u>third</u> form of consciousness is that of a universal '<u>collective mind</u>' of consciousness. Perhaps something of the nature of the universal concepts of reality which we derive from and share in common with the family and tribe into which we are born and raised. That is to say, transmitted to us by the culture of our society.

A part of both individual and collective mind is the <u>collective memory</u> of the community. The British as well as the Gallic Druids committed their laws as well as their learning to memory. It was the first legal archive. Preservation of verse and music as mnemonic devices attests to the special importance of memory in the days before the printed book. (p. 483 Boorstin's, *The Discoverers*)

Yet, there are rules, laws, and equations of quantum physics and theory that constrains the parameters of our any reality. To propose and act toward goals beyond the limits of quantum theory, is but an exercise in futility.

-Abstract by RGB-

* * * * *

Experiment In Consciousness

I am reminded of my strange experience of some thirty five years ago on a very quiet Sunday morning when I had slept-in. My wife of those times had dragged the children off to her church-which is why it was so unusually quiet that day. The instant I awoke to consciousness I became aware that I did not know who I was; nor where I was. My first impulse was to open my eyes, to gather clues from my surroundings as to who and where I was. But I resolved to resist that impulse. Nor was there a sound ("there wasn't a breath in that land of death") available to clue me in. I intended from pure intense effort of recollection, alone-to summon forth to my consciousness the details of my past and present. I supposed that a single clue would then cascade all of that into my accustomed waking state of awareness. I awaited a long while. As best I can recall, that first clue was finally an external faint auditory clue to remind me where I be. In the blink of an eye, my accustomed state of consciousness was again cascaded upon me. And I op'ed mine eyes to reaffirm my first impression.

One might suppose that an instinct for **language** and the force of reason have been infused deeply into the subconscious, such that when required, it can be summoned up into the processes of one's consciousness or comes forth automatically-as does a function such as breathing. Yet, in that transient pre-awakening state, I thought it curious that my being was disconnected from all memories of my personhood-which I yet supposed to reside separately elsewhere in my now yet untapped subconscious mind. Also, I was in that brief moment of revelry, comfortably isolated from sensory perceptions of touch, taste, smell, vision and auditory stimulus. It was as though I were dealing with a primitive sense of singular being and consisting almost entirely of vague curiosity. Who? Why? What? Where? When? How?

The situation must have had somewhat in common with that of a newborn in its first few days after birth upon opening its eyes to the dawn of its 'being'. The earliest stages of awaking. Except that (in the above cited incident) I had a language with which I could converse and reason within myself and was able to formulate a plan to deal with this situation as a learning opportunity. And a well-honed experienced capacity to tap instantly into a well developed matured state of awareness and readiness.

Compare the suddenness of awakening from sleep, to the much slower gradual awakening from post-surgical anesthesia. And to the very much slower and often incomplete recovery following coma and brain swelling caused by head injury. The fullness of consciousness is always a matter of degree.

The more we understand the world around us, the more conscious one can become.

⁕　⁕　⁕　⁕　⁕

Language And Consciousness

There is no vocal conversation without consciousness, nor without a language. Nor without a culture, for even among human beings, language cannot come into existence without an intercommunication with other minds of one's milieu.

Is even consciousness perhaps physical? Or not physical but something we call conceptual, 'mental', and intangible? Consciousness can be said to be perhaps the most important component of one's individual personal conceptual universe.

And consciousness is very much benefited by the co-existence of the ever present subconscious aspect of mind. The subconscious being: that which an individual does not or will not recognize as a component of his conscious psyche. A subconscious which could almost be conceived of as a shirking of a part of one's task of fully appreciating just what sort of a person one thinks himself to be. And even one's consciousness can fail to recognize whether one's symptoms are real or imaginary; and fail to recognize one's own frame of mind, for example.

※　※　※　※　※

Subconscious Component Of Mind

Consciousness implies memory as well as self-awareness. But let us abstract ourselves from the reality of the extant world.

Yes, we have come each to be fully aware of our conscious mind through the waking hours of our every day lives. A matter of major curiosity though, is how little we become aware of the vast subconscious component of mind. For its function and its content are the supporting foundation upon which the intense flame of our small bit of conscious awareness is fully dependent. The conscious aspect of our life is like unto the capstone of the massive base of a large pyramid that we might liken unto the content of the subconscious. From infancy, day by day, we consciously and subconsciously acquire new information and mature the know-how of our every little bodily skill. How to attain a sitting position, how to hold a spoon and feed ourselves, how to tie a shoelace, how to throw a ball, how to ride a bike, how to call in an ordered sequence of muscular action to produce the beauty of walking stride or a dance performance. All are intricate skills that we nurture by long practice into the subconscious where they are retained and which in unerring anticipation come forth automatically to serve the moment-by-moment intentions and plans of one's waking consciousness.

And in our waking lives, not for a single moment is our activity of decision allowed to rest. It takes a strong act of will to try not to talk to yourself when you're walking down the street says Noam Chomsky. Even when in desperation we abandon ourselves to whatever may happen, we have decided not to decide.

From the realm of the <u>sub</u>conscious, we awake each morning to find ourselves bathed in rich and wondrous sensations which connect us to That-Which-Is" of the external world of reality. And to the odd phenomenon of our own individual physical being; within which these perceptions are come to lodge. That again is consciousness. A consciousness which is of an always limited and variable degree from person to person; and from moment to moment within one's own state of fluctuating wellness and of wakefulness. We too continuously change and evolve. "A poem is never finished, it is only abandoned and always yet unfinished." Neither is a life ever completed to fulfillment-always comes too early to its demise. "When we remember that we are all mad, the mysteries disappear and life stands explained", says Mark Twain.

✳   ✳   ✳   ✳   ✳

From our knowledge and awareness of the world about us, we are led to infer that conscious awareness in its highest degree is possessed by our species, Homo sapiens. But we recognize lesser degrees of consciousness among animate creatures far on down in the genetic tree of life.

ANIMALS
I think I could turn and live with animals.
They are so placid and self contained.
. . . .
They do not sweat and whine about their condition.
They do not lie awake in the dark and weep for their sins.
They do not make me sick discussing their duty to God.
Not one is dissatisfied-not one is demented

with the mania of owning things.
Not one kneels to another, nor to one of his kind
that lived thousands of years ago.
Not one is respectable or industrious over the whole earth.
Walt Whitman

Among the living animalcule we note for example that those ancient creatures we call ants seem to have acquired the ability to live in perfect harmony among their own civilizations. They seem as though perhaps to possess no individual personality, mentality, or ego, as they go about their ordered routine. Seem as though to have no fears or moral scruples and rarely hesitate as though to be in the throws of dilemma-except when obstructed with obvious physical impediments. The whole pattern of their individual lives seems as though to have been entirely set and fixed to them through their genetic inheritance. (reflexes + instincts) But even they would seem to possess at least some little conscious awareness.

And among plants, those that we categorize as weeds seem to have the heartiest of survival powers and efficiency of existence. They might be seen to have this ability in consequence of wasting none of their energy in the production of fruit or flower; but rather by concentrating all their energies into the production of multitudes of durable seed. (Wilson)

What in one's being is higher than consciousness? Consciousness (a component of 'mind' and 'f of CNS') is a quality of fluctuating intensity varying from a lethargic baseline of mere wakefulness just above unconsciousness, to a highly attentive state and focused thought, for example, upon the working out of a problem in Algebra or Geometry. Consciousness is a characteristic or attribute of our conceptual notion of 'the mind'. Dependent upon and entwined with a personal history in the recollections or memories of one's 'mind'. Consciousness implies memory as well as self-awareness. "For there is no (focused) perception that is not full of memories"-says Henry Bergson.

* * * * *

On Memory

Memory And Imagination

The word 'memory' by conventional usage is suggestive of an accurate recollection. Whereas in fact, some sort of an embellishment of that recollection in the short term memory is required even to elevate that recollection into the long-term memory system. The memory has thus already become an altered recollection on that basis alone.

The mental abilities that we call intellect and imagination would seem to be closely connected to, and dependent upon memory. And there would appear to be qualities of memory that vary in intensity from vague, to vivid. Additionally, there are two separate types of memory-short-term memory and long-term memory. Of short-term memory, only a portion is selected and passed on into long-term memory. In particular, that which we judge to be 'significant', and often, that which is tinged and coated with various qualities of emotion (from out of our past experience) or are reinforced by information from more than one sensory modality. These modalities being also of various intensity in the impressions they make upon our powers of the mind.

In this civilized world, certainly even every young child and adult human being is acquainted with the concept of imagination, and is quite aware themselves of having very much exercised their own imaginations on a regular basis.

"There is a linguistic oddity in the fact that there exists a general tendency to ascribe some sort of other-worldly reality to the imaginary.

And then to treat of minds as though they were the clandestine habitats of these intangible objects and pseudo-scenarios of one's fantasy." (Ryle) But mind itself is only a non-tangible conception which though it functions in time, does not exist in space. Hence, mind is not a place, and the objects and scenarios of fantasy are also not reality-they are only things in the category of intangible ideas. Distinctly different and separate from the tangible objects and objective scenarios of the outer tangible world into which our tangible bodies have been relegated. Tangible bodies which are in communication and interaction through our motor and sensory nervous system with the tangible world of reality. A sensory system which feeds information as sensations into the CNS to produce our impressions. A real world where objects and scenarios exist in both time and space. An always tangibly threatening and potentially dangerous real world.

"It was Hume's mistaken thought that both (sensations and images) were real." (p. 249 Ryle) "Or that perceptions were of two types-namely, impressions and the ghosts or echoes of impressions." Images of the mind however are not real in that though they occur in time, they do not occur in space but rather only in the intangible mind.

Imaginings, of course are exercises of one's mental powers, though they do not exist in the real world. Those mental 'exercises' are of course powered by tangible neurons and neuronal nets of the CNS. <u>Imaginings are in fact even a part of the mind's process of rational thought</u>. Of use in soliloquy for example, to allow one to ponder and consider possible consequences before endangering ourselves with rash action. If 'A' and if 'B', then 'C'.

That people speak of seeing things 'in their mind's eye' or hearing things in their head, is not proof that there actually exist 'in their heads' these things that they 'see' and 'hear'. No more than a staged murder has an actual victim.

A part of our wish and fantasy world (from the realm of ideas) we may repetitively ruminate up into organized and workable conceptual ideas. Ideas which we might call 'dreams' and aspiration for our possible attainment in the real world of our bodily existence. Motivation. An example of how the intangible realm of idea is able to influence a tangible body of and in a tangible world of reality. More than any other creature of the real world, mankind is gifted with the rational intangible mind. A gift in addition to, and even above reflexes and instincts, that has enabled mankind to attain status near the very top of the feeding chain. And facilitates one's elusiveness when threatened. A gift that has gradually enabled mankind even to modify the very surface of the planet to better serve his well-being and comforts of life. A gift that has finally enabled him to aspire, accomplish, and achieve to goals and purposes beyond nature's basic mandates of birth, struggle, reproduction, and death.

❊   ❊   ❊   ❊   ❊

Recent scientific investigation suggests that the process of memory formation requires the formation of new neurons in the hippocampus. Here, thousands of new neurons are produced each week from precursor stem cells. Many of these promptly become incorporated into the circuitry of the hippocampus. And we are told that if sleep and dreaming are experimentally prevented, memory formation and the formation of new neurons in the hippocampus are seriously impaired. A rational to fully justify a therapeutic intervention for sleep disorders.

In almost all of the rest of the brain, new neurons are never formed. So that if cortical neurons (with which we are born) get damaged, the cortex cannot repair itself. (p. 109 John Young)

From memory comes the potential for <u>creative imagination</u>. A form of fiction. Capacity to recall the past enables and encourages one to imagine the future. (see Hybrow) Our wandering daily ruminations include such things as our fears, our wishes, our desires, our hopes, and our expectations. In short, such things as can trigger the creative imagination into a fantasy. And the creative embellishment of fantasies can be a positive motivating factor to a person living a balanced and well proportioned life. Can through repetition evolve into dreams (in the sense of aspirations for a more complete self-fulfillment towards which one may strive-a long term project). Yet can sometimes devolve into obsessive ideation and delusions to a destabilized or an unbalanced mind.

There is a certain pleasure to be had from one's indulgence in imaginative 'day-dreams'. The taste of which is common to all. To create in fancy with one's own imagination though pleasant to some degree, falls short of an actual experience such as might resolve or satisfy one's whim or desire. As a few drops of water are not apt to quench a deep thirst. Therefore, a scenario of imagination does not ever quite free one from the grip of one's wishful fantasy. May tend perhaps to become obsessively recurrent. While to act out that wishful fantasy into reality holds greater promise of giving temporary psychic relief-or an actual satiation or sense of fulfillment.

In the matter of memory and self-knowledge there appear to be two separate but parallel brain process. (see Ashworth) The first of these is named as 'reflexive thought' and which seems to involve the amygdala (the seat of emotion), the basal ganglia (which seems to be the base of one's habitual bodily motion processes) and the ventral medial areas of the prefrontal cortex (which evaluates, plans, and executes one's intentions of habitual bodily activity). Its use of memory is in a superficial gathering of "the-gist-of-a-matter". This reflexive thought would seem to be preconscious, rapid, automatic, and effortless. And of use especially, for example, in an athletic performance. These built-in reflexes are the 'inherent knowledge' of which Plato is speaking. They are the behavioral reflexes and instincts of genetic memories about the experiences of earlier ancestral brains. They would appear to be programmed by genetic DNA coded to a person in a chemical form. (p. 112 Blakemore)

But it is inconceivable that the empirical experiences of each individual animal is actually represented by the synthesis or alteration of molecules. Expressions of innate reflexes too, require the construction of nerve pathways.

But there is a second, and conscious form of thought which is slow, and requires one's focused effort of attention in gathering data from one's memory; and expecting a form of evidence-based learning into one's consciousness. It appears to involve the lateral prefrontal cortex (executive function), the hippocampus (seat of memory), the medial temporal lobe, and a posterior parietal area of the cortex. This form of mental activity is more useful to deep thought and contemplation as in intellectual performance.

❊   ❊   ❊   ❊   ❊

Photographic Memory?

Ability to delay gratification appears to be a primary predictor of adult IQ. A matter of one's acquiring self discipline. Teaching ourselves to think so that we can outsmart desires. One must learn to use the attentive mind-just as one must learn to use a computer. Accuracy and capacity of memory would also seem to be useful parameters by which to measure of a person's I.Q. Which brings to the subject of photographic memory.

To begin with, it is to be noted that "people are apt grossly to exaggerate the photographic fidelity of their visual imagery." (p. 275 Ryle)

Since my teenage years I have intermittently heard it said that an occasional person has a 'photographic memory'. Namely, persons of high intellect and most commonly perhaps to be those who were known to be quite good students in school. I understood that to mean that such a person possessed unusually good memory. That everything in which they took interest enough to read and study of, they could subsequently conjure up unerringly into their memory as lines of writing or print, everything they had read on this or that subject. That they could for example look at a letter or a page briefly, and then subsequently conjure up an image of that in their 'minds eye' and recount that information in complete and perfect detail. As though able to re-read the contents of that page directly from an image that they were holding before their 'minds-eye'. The said page, and the said 'minds-eye' as though existing and functioning somewhere within their CNS. An ability they might use quite to their personal advantage over their fellow schoolmates, to facilitate the ease with which they could outperform us ordinary mortals in all of their schoolwork and tests. Generally therefore they were apt to be near the top of their class in GPA. Class valedictorian and salutatorian, perhaps.

But though thus gifted with that ability, they might also be lazy and lethargic, so that they might not trouble themselves much or often to exercise their intellectual talent. Might perhaps be more interested in frittering away their time as clever pranksters and involving themselves in devious schemes. Predisposed at times to wander into illegalities. To become perhaps a gifted shoplifter or crook.

My older brother was said by some to have had one of these photographic memories. He was an unusually good student all through college, medical school, and residency training. He very much impressed me with his intellect and much influenced the course of my own life. I can't recall if he ever directly informed me of his being in possession of a photographic mind, but such was my understanding as iterated to me from other sources.

I never had cause to look at his report cards from school, but as far as I know, he was not at the top of his class in high school. And yet, I have heard that he was called 'the brain'. I do know for a fact that he was a prolific reader since his early grade school years and throughout his life. Though he seemed to be very healthy and athletic, he did not take part in any athletic programs while he was in school. He would never have had the time for that. Poverty was our lot in those years and he occupied himself with odd jobs since he was perhaps nine or 10 years of age. During his two years in the Navy he was in the signal Corps, and he kept a daily journal, many of whose pages I have perused in years past.

Immediately after two years in the Navy, he registered in premedical college courses. And in each summer break, he always found work either with the railroad or in construction. And once married and into his professional career, one might find him usually at home and reading in his spare time. In short, there seems no need to suppose that he had any short-cuts to knowledge such as a photographic mind. His wide grasp of knowledge and information might as readily be explained simply on the basis of his continuous reading on a wide variety of subjects through many years. But yes, one might suppose it possible that he also had a photographic mind-whatever that is-if there ever were such a thing.

I had a high school classmate with whom I was acquainted through grade school and high school, who was very well-read, informed, and at the top of our class in those years. He was valedictorian of our graduating class. He was said to have a photographic memory-whatever that is. What I do not know about him is just how much time he spent reading. He did not spend time in school athletics or even in band or chorus. I never saw him to be wandering the streets aimlessly and he was not engaged in after-school jobs to my awareness. I am tempted and left to presume that he read a lot.

If there are those with 'photographic memories', there are undoubtedly some who commonly go to school managing to earn only average grades, but without having ever to exert themselves with much effort. I recently became interested in this business of photographic minds when I was informed by a grandson that he regards himself as having a photographic mind. He does seem to perform well in learning tasks when he puts his mind to it.

Now, there do appear to be those who can demonstrate remarkable feats of memory-as well as of creative imagination. Some, I suppose, because their particular family or social background encourages stimulation of memory so that they end up with a predisposition to good memory out of habit-along with the habit of much reading. Obviously, or course, nothing can come forth from even the best of anyone's memory except and <u>unless it has first gotten into the memory by experience, reading, or word-of-mouth.</u>

There are also those who demonstrate a talent for good memory by honing a practiced method of power of recall as a sort of stunt with which to wow the folks. The question is, whether they are only stunts for enlarging the capacity for short-term memory, or rather, are they actually getting information into long-term memory?

My life experience and information leads me to conclude that though a great deal of information passes through short-term memory, yet only a small portion of that passes into the long-term memory. And that of that information, ideas, or concepts which is presented to short-memory, one generally only then recalls 'the gist of the thing'. And only rarely would be able to reiterate the content of an explanation in word for word recollection. Again, as if to imply that most of the trivial details presented to the memory are weeded out, as though irrelevant to the purposes of long-term memory.

In our human species, visual observation has preeminence over our other sensory modalities. And for most people therefore, visual imagination is stronger than auditory, kinesthetic, tactile, taste, or touch imagination. The limitations of our language is such that persons will often speak of 'visualizing' things, but we have no corresponding words for imagery of the other sorts.

Again, in considering the notion of a photographic-memory, persons are often heard to say that they can still picture in their 'minds-eye' the image of a departed friend or relative. But the mind has no access to any secondary inner image. One must presume that like myself, their memory can retain some particularly prominent features or mannerisms of the person of their regard. I too have access to such vague images to my recollection, but they certainly are rather ghostly and threadbare resemblances. And as we recede in time from actual interaction with a friend or loved one, our ability to conjure up any sort of image of that person's appearance dims and gradually fades.

From my memory I might be enabled to draw a picture on paper of that person such as might finally resemble that persons appearance. Just as a skilled artist on the street corner might be able rapidly to produce a picture of a passerby in the space of a minute or two by observing and reproducing the person's prominent features to end up with something akin to a cartoon that might resemble the person of regard. Given a much longer 'sitting' of the subject of one's artistic ability, the drawing or depiction is apt to demonstrate a much greater resemblance. But even the experienced artist will never end up with a drawing that exactly depicts the object person of regard. The critic will always easily discern the mighty dissimilarity between the painting or drawing from the person of regard when they are placed together in close proximity.

For one to claim that he can still conjure up a vivid image of a person in his minds eye is at the same time to acknowledge that his inner picture is not quite accurate. Persons describing a particular visual memory not uncommonly express that memory with a saying such as "I fancy that I can vividly see his angry appearance and demeanor". thereby doubly admitting the fiction of there being any 'photographic memory'. For 'fancy' is a word derived from the word fantasy. And the word 'vividly' suggests a quality of less than real. And recognized by the person as not actual. And he can almost invariably acknowledge the qualitative difference. Save only in situations of metabolically intoxicated, damaged, or psychotic brains. Memory is not all that we consciously are, but, almost so. Once beyond infancy and early childhood, "there is no perception that is not full of memories", [Bergson]

In consciousness we are the entire set of memories and concepts that we acquire (along with the skills and talents we have acquired through repetitive action, practice, and experience.) Including also the innate reflexes and instincts which we have acquired genetically. Every one of our newly acquired memories changes who we are-(p. 34 *Discover* Mag April 4, 2012) Instead of being a perfect movie of the past, memory is more like a shifting collage-a narrative spun out of scraps and constructed anew whenever a recollection takes place. (p. 65 Dyson) And there occurs a reconsolidation of a memory after each recital. Unless or until at least, it can be recited on a word-by-word basis-as one memorizes a poem.

✳   ✳   ✳   ✳   ✳

Altered Memory

The cognitive mind function and it's memory can be said to have a "story building process in which the past is reworked and then returned in its altered state into storage" in memory. The repeated cycles allow the brain to hold onto only small but shrinking fragments of these former conscious states.

The remembering of one's story of what happened is always at least a somewhat altered memory. Though an object or situation be perceived, there is yet most commonly a failure to grasp some essential detail of the event in question.

"Over a lifetime the details of real events are increasingly distorted by editing and supplementation. Across generations the most important among them turn into history, and finally into legend, and myth." (pp. 132-133 Wilson)

If the conscious mind is not at the center of the motive and analytic action in the brain, it is perhaps right at its immediate perimeter? (p. 49, The Week, Dec 30, 2011) Working memory- consists of the limited information we are able consciously to consider at any given moment in the spotlight of one's immediate but limited momentary awareness.

A smiling face triggers an "approach response in the perceptions of one who perceives it at either a conscious or sub-conscious level." The content of the subconscious seems to have its influence on one even while one's immediate consciousness is not aware of it.

One can make an attempt to record a written record of a dream. But as one begins to enter it into the notebook, it is noticed to be quite incomplete, and we find ourselves bridging gaps and improbabilities with what seems more probable, or at least with something from one's imagination to complete a coherent 'recital' of one's recollection of some now uncertain dream event. Memory and imagination are two sides of one coin, as it were. As illustrated by the following:

Some twenty or thirty years ago there were a rash of reports, accounts, and stories suggesting and leading to sensational charges of 'heinous child abuse' having been perpetrated by the staffers of various child-care facilities. Such for example of a case of The Little Rascals daycare center for children somewhere in North Carolina. I am given to understand that there were similar localities across the county where such similar things were getting attention. I am more familiar with the specific instance of the situation that transpired in Wenatchee, WA, having at one time read the details of the matter as I was writing an essay on the subject (An essay upon which I cannot now put my finger). I had read the details of the Wenatchee situation in a book, (*Satanism*, by Tamara L. Rolf). My high school classmate, Lynn F. tells me that his son was caught up and accused in a similar situation in Portland. Says it cost him a lot of time and money to get the son exculpated from those bogus accusations.

These were not trivial occurrences. Thorough-going and prolonged investigations were launched and the juvenile courts were involved in the handling of a host of odd allegations. Satanic rituals and devil worship were among the accusations, as well as sexual improprieties visited upon the young children by the day care staffers. And allegations against clergymen in whose church building these day-care centers were located. Some of the accused ended up in prison.

From whence did the 'evidence' for these actual court cases arise? "Out of the mouths of babes", so it seems. Social workers and gullible police officers with 'special experience with juveniles' on these such matters had 'suspicions' of these dark doings. And they had access to and custody of these youngsters.

As to how these suspicions arose?? Presumably they had heard and read of previous such allegations in reading old information on witchcraft out of medieval Europe and then in Salem, Mass. And now, a couple of centuries later, a newly begotten professional copycat fad had been resurrected. Dug up-from a nearly forgotten episode of the foolishness of times past. Overdrafts of wide-spread suspicions said to be based on the reality of their experience (of perhaps the reality of... yes-the actual occasional pedophile).

In each such locality where these alleged absurdities were evolving, a little nidus of these suspicious professionals would seem to have reinforced one another's suspicions. Overly zealous and imaginative social workers, 'special' police officers as well as the judges have regular cause to interact among themselves, and with the youth in "Juvenile Justice Systems" courts. Soon, the imaginations of one or a few such judges too were fired by a clustering of these accusations of 'trained professionals' concerning these delusional heinous mysteries of dark doings in their midst. Had even the judges forgotten the lessons of the Salem witchcraft debacle?

In any case, these sorts of 'professionals' were all involved and schooled by one another in techniques for planting, worming-out, and elaborating darkly suspicious details from the pre-school age memories of befuddled children.

To recall is a feat at which we sometimes must put forth a mighty mental effort.

Memories, or imagination? Two sides of the same coin. Young children pumped repeatedly for information. With each recitation, opportunity anew for the injection of the new and fortification of the old mistaken details into the bewildered and infirm memories of children. And reconsolidated there as the ever new version of immature memories. Cleverly suggestive 'diagnostic techniques' with 'anatomically correct dolls' (specifically with touchable private parts) and suggestive drawings to aid the youngsters in how to pin-the-tail-on-the-donkey, as it were.

In the juvenile courts, "special rules of evidence" were implemented (as in the Salem witchcraft trials). The testimony of suspected and accused adults was ever under deep suspicion. The 'evidence' that seemed to have standing was that of 'twice-told-tales' from the mouths of confused children. Fragments of 'information' coaxed from young children which was pieced together and iterated as 'evidence' by these imaginative juvenile case workers and 'special' juvenile police officers. Implicit memory is entirely separate from explicit memories

It would be interesting to discover what has become of all of these misguided social workers, policemen, and judges now, after all these years since this baloney has been largely debunked and mostly forgotten. Well meaning intentions perhaps? once more "gang oft astray". Overly zealous 'public servants' inciting one another's delusions? Malicious mischief?

✳   ✳   ✳   ✳   ✳

Mirror Cells

Which brings us next to another speculative theory-**a Mirror Cell System**. (p. 92 Colapinto) By which is meant a network circuit system in the CNS that gradually enables one to see himself as others may be perceiving him. Enables one to psychically put himself into the shoes of another from time to time. From that perspective does he thus recognize in himself, the presence of his own mind and its traits of consciousness and self-consciousness. A system that would appear to be highly dependent in its evolution on the existence of a language by which persons can communicate their thoughts and ideas to one another.

Interestingly there is a form of childhood Schizophrenia known as Autism, in which the child become withdrawn and seems to be lacking in the ability to communicate effectively with those about him. Makes little eye contact and seems to have but little use for affection, his intellect being prepossessed by his own solitary games and imagination. As though he possessed no mirror cell system.

✳   ✳   ✳   ✳   ✳

Anatomy and Physiology of CNS

Need For Food And Rest

One's conscious awareness requires a considerable quantity of continuous energy, which is metabolically generated by the brain (CNS) of one's structurally intact CNS. 20% of the calories one consumes are consumed in the CNS. So limited and tenuous is the supply of that energy requirement (to the maintenance of full consciousness), that the brain is unable to supply enough energy on a continuous basis. It would appear that conscious thought is expensive; but that there must occur a subconscious mental processing which is perhaps more economical.

Like the battery of my lap-top computer, the brain's store of energy declines through the hours of its usage each day and comes to require an interval of 'down time' for a recharging. Brain function must have rest. Sleep deprivation is sometimes imposed as a form of torture and punishment. Un-imposed insomnia is also a torture. Were one to be deprived for but two weeks of opportunity for sleep, death soon ensues. 25 to 35% of people are said to have insomnia problems and it tends to be more common with increasing age. Insomnia is said often to be associated with anxiety, which from my personal experience and in common sense is unquestionably the case. Suggestive that anti-anxiety medication may be therapeutically useful in treating insomnia.

"Nothing in all the range of human complaints excites my sympathy so much as sleeplessness. The eternal inescapable sleepless night", (says Hertzler, in *"The Horse and Buggy Doctor"*). People long for sleep. The deeper the better. They do what they can from what little is available to them to facilitate sleep. Folks tend to ruminate on their wearisome repetitive compulsive fears, concerns, regrets, delusions, and scenarios. The effort of analysis if not otherwise beyond their mental powers, is unattainable in the face of their mental fatigue. Comforting hopes and wishes stir the morass of their unresolved chaotic thought to no avail. Sleeplessness remains. Extreme physical exhaustion might bring some sleep. So might alcohol and many other substances which are readily available. All such have unwanted various collateral side effects. Some substances are available through the local physician-but people can become dependent and may then be in need of a cure from dependency. By way of banishing the occasional and sometimes chronic forms of sleeplessness, there is always the search for the substance that will facilitate the state of restful sleep-with the least possible of adverse side affects.

How many nights have I too, ended up with my abandonment of the attempt to sleep-lest I find myself returned to the disturbing dream from which I have escaped into wakefulness; or entangled in some repetitious ruminations of mere semi-sleep?

Awareness of the external environment must be shut off during sleep-to gain the chance to integrate new and old memories. (pp. 34-39 Sc. Amer. Aug 2013) "If sleep does not serve an absolutely vital function, then it is the biggest mistake the evolutionary process has ever made." says Allan Rechtschaffe, pioneer of 'Sleep Science'.

Why do people and animals sleep? The question has long puzzled scientists and sparked several competing theories. A new study on mice claims to have suggested an answer: The brain physically cleans itself during sleep, essentially running a nightmare rinse cycle that flushes out the CNS toxic waste products of its metabolism which have build up during the day. "The brain has only a limited energy at its disposal and it appears that it must choose between two different functional states-awake-and-aware; or asleep and in a clean-up mode." This, from Univ. of Rochester neurologist M.N. who tells BBC.com that she has found that during sleep, the cells in a mouse's CNS shrink dramatically, increasing the space between them by some 60%. That allows cerebral-spinal-fluid (CSF) to circulate more freely and wash away extra-cellular waste. Each day ¼ oz. and in the course of each month, ½ lb. of detritus needs must be flushed away. (p. 26 Nedergaard) Upon waking, the brain cells again enlarge and the CSF flow slows again to a trickle. Among the residue removed from the brain during sleep is beta-amyloid, a plaque-forming substance that is said to be a hallmark of Alzheimers Dementia. M.N. says it is probably no coincidence that diseases associated with dementia are linked to sleep disorders, raising the possibility that adequate sleep may be important in slowing the progression of brain damage. (p. 19 "The Week" November 8, 2013) Those who are chronically sleep-deprived also have increased risks of heart disease, obesity, and early death. (p. 15 Sc. Amer. Sept. 2013)

There is no lymphatic system to serve the CNS as there is for the other tissues of the body. But recently there is some suggestion that the astrocytes of the CNS actually do perform a function that is comparable to that of the lymphatic system.

In my professional experience I have encountered many a patient in some state or another of dementia, but I am reminded most vividly by my closer observations and reflections of my mother and a brother as each slowly to sank into a progressive state of senility. I remember particularly how my mother was eventually cut off from her connection to her use of words and language. Though she seemed yet attentive to us, her kin, and what was going on about her, yet she then exhibited an anguishing frustration at her own unsuccessful attempt to express to us what she had on her mind.

✻ ✻ ✻ ✻ ✻

Brain And Mind

What we know as the human brain, is considered to be the most "recently" phylo-genetically evolved among all species. The brain lies atop of and has extensive neuronal connection to and through the brain-stem which consists of the mid-brain and the hind-brain (medulla) through which the neurons of the cerebrum are in connection and functionally integrated with the spinal chord and the peripheral nervous system. An arrangement that provides the chemical-electric stimulus and coordination to the body's musculature mechanisms-thus making the body the servant to the needs, wishes, and desires of (the functions of) the brain which we call "the mind".

The function of the brain is in the gathering and managing of information. It functions in the acquisition, storage, and retrieval of information; and in the selecting and choosing among alternative bits of information. A reconnoitering of the social and physical landscapes of the real world such as to aid our facility in the transiting of those territories in our journey through life.

"Perception, learning, and action comprise the fundamental engine of the mind." (see Highbrow) The brain is protectively enclosed within the bony skull and its metabolic functions are supported by the heart and vascular system with which oxygen from the lungs and nutrients from the digestive system are supplied.

The brain is an organ of about 3 pounds in weight (representing about 2% of the total weight of an adult person). Its cortex covers an area three times larger than in a chimpanzee. This highly convoluted cerebral cortex (gray matter) is a dense collection of 30 billion cell bodies stacked to a depth of 1/5 an inch thick, whose various areas represent sensory, motor, and association (communication) functions. (see Ashwell)

Each half of the symmetrically divided brain is subdivided into lobes:

Frontal lobe related primarily to executive functions. Occipital lobe related primarily vision.
Temporal lobe related primarily to hearing.
Parietal lobes are involved in a number of important functions in the body. They seem also to receive significant input from the Occipital and Temporal lobes and thus are especially important to one's sense of spatial orientation. The somato-sensory cortex is found within the

parietal lobes. It receives and process sensory information from all over the body and helps us to identify objects by touch. The somato-sensory cortex helps us to identify the location of a touch sensation and to discriminate between sensations such as temperature and pain. Neurons in the parietal lobes also receive touch, visual and other sensory information from a part of the brain called the thalamus. The thalamus relays nerve signals and sensory information between the peripheral nervous system and the cerebral cortex.

The frontal-parietal network connections may be central to the experience of consciousness. The work of concentrated organized analytical thought of one's conscious life is expensive. Work that functionally synchronizes and binds together nerve cells in diverse regions of the brain. 20% of the calories consumed by each person of our species are expended in the CNS. A considerably larger proportion than any other species. And still, with the brain in continuous conversation with itself day and night, the subconscious is said to consume 80% of the brain's daily energy requirement. (see Hybrow)

There are said to be 100 trillion synaptic connections of intern-neuronal communication between these cortical cells. These appear to form the multitude of functional neural networks which underlie the coordination of the multiple tasks for which the brain is responsible, in their united efforts in giving rise to that intangible function which we designate as the human mind. Functions such as memory, imagination, observation, evaluation, calculation, judgment, cognition, consciousness, motivation to action etc. Functions that charge our inner lives with positive and negative emotions which themselves are motivating factors in human behavior and response to our covert inner and overt outer lives. It is postulated that our memories (cognits) each persist within a separate network. Each network being a collaboration of interconnected neurons. It would seem that each such gestalt is continuously subject to refinement or reinforcement by the ongoing experience of our lives. It is said that we possess a perception/action cycle; in that we perceive what we remember-and remember what we perceive.

It would seem to be our conscious and focused attention to stimuli by which (in large measure) we adapt and adjust to the outer world and universe; and to relate to one another. And yet, we are also hard-wired neurologically with built-in reflexes which initiate and control much or our bodily responsiveness to both inner and outer stimuli. Thus, it would have to be said that while on the one hand much of our animal bodily response to stimuli is dictated solely by that which is neurologically tangible within us. Yet the "mind" (which is intangible) very much overshadows the reflexive component of our human nature, and is the major contributor to what it is that makes we of the Homo sapiens species into god-like conscious, sentient, social, and moral beings.

42% of the adult brain is said to be composed of mostly insulating myelinated connecting axons from and between cells of the gray matter. The myelin greatly enhances the speed and efficiency of brain function. The non-myelinated axons are said to conduct electricity at only 20 mph, whereas the myelinated fiber conducts at a speed of 270 mph. At birth the process of myelination is only begun, and that process is not completed until the early or mid-20 years of age. This matter of an immature brain is, in fact, reflected in the reality of their immature minds. Society has long recognized and made allowances for that reality in its lesser expectations and legal permissiveness related to the chronological age of our youth. (see Highbrow)

✳   ✳   ✳   ✳   ✳

"A Confederacy Of Senses"
by Lawrence Rosenblum
Abstract by RGB

Neuroscientists and psychologists have largely abandoned early notions that the brain is similar to a Swiss Army knife in which distinct regions are dedicated to different senses. It seems rather that the brain has evolved to encourage as much cross-talk as possible between the senses. It appears that the sensory regions of the brain are much physically intertwined.

In 1970 the FBI began a program of lip reading. Lip reading is actually a talent that we all rely upon-much more than we realize. The senses collaborate even more than previously realized.

The ability to understand one another is diminished if we cannot see the lips of the speaker as he speaks. Especially so, in a noisy environment or if the speech is derived from a person with a thick accent. The learning of lip–reading is an important part of typical speech development. It has been noted that blind infants take longer to learn various aspects of speech, and that their visual cortexes tend to rewire themselves for speech. There seems to be an automaticity in this rewiring. We simply cannot help but integrate the words we see on another's lips with the words that we hear from those lips. Multi-sensory speech perception has helped to bring about a revolution in our understanding of how the brain organizes the information it receives from our several different senses.

It seems that our several senses are always eavesdropping on one another. A life-long predisposition and custom such as continuously to verify, to add details, to correct, and upgrade one's ongoing world-view of the nature of one's ever evolving perceptive reality.

A sighted person being blindfolded for even just one half hour becomes extra sensitive to touch via the visual cortex. And brain scans have shown that the visual cortex of blind persons do rewire visual cortex for hearing. And it has been shown among persons engaged in lip-face research, that it similarity fires up the auditory cortex. Research of the past 50 years demonstrates that no sense modality works alone.

Blind–deaf persons such as Helen Keller have shown themselves capable of interpreting someone's speech by placing their fingers on a person's lips, cheeks, and neck. Further experimentation suggests that the brain may give equal weight to speech gleaned from ears, eyes, and even the skin-not to say that these distinct modalities provide an equal amount of information. Implying only that the brain makes concerted effort to consider and combine all the different types of speech information.

The several distinct senses help one another process the same type of information. The specific manner in which a person speaks seems to provide information about the person who is speaking. There is no doubt that the distinct modes of one's perception are combined and entangled in the brain.

The brain does not channel visual information from the eyes into one container; and auditory information from ears into another discrete container as though it were sorting coins. Rather, our brains derive meaning from the world in as many ways as possible by blending the diverse forms of sensory perception. And it does turn out that making the effort to read someone's lips does improve one's ability to hear that person's spoken words, even against a background of random noise.

Magnificent though the sensory system function be, yet each of the five senses is very limited as to what information it can supply to one's conscious mind concerning the infinite reality of the world and universe in which we exist and have our being. "The cure for the shortcomings of our senses is not to stop using them, but to use them critically and to be aware of there shortcomings." (p. 30 Abel) And a single source of information can by no means report as accurately to one's understanding as can be two or even more sensory sources of information. With five senses we are much better equipped to explore the manifold unknowns of what we soon come to recognize as being the very intricate and vast unknown reality of the world and universe.

On Vision

The visual sense is indeed the major contributory of sensory information to the CNS and as such, its integration into the CNS underlies and produces functional information to that intangible process 'mind', (which is a function of CNS'). One might reasonably declare that "visual observation has pre-eminence" over input of the other senses. (p. 247 Ryle) Thus, "for most people, visual imagination is stronger than auditory, tactual, kinesthetic, olfactory, and gustatory imagination. And consequently, the language in which we discuss these matters is largely drawn from the language of seeing. People speak, for example, of picturing or visualizing things, but they have no corresponding generic verbs for modes of other sensory inputs." (p. 247 Ryle)

One may raise the question as to how purely electrical signals from the eyes to the visual cortex can be converted into that which is suggested as being a pictorial image in our 'minds eye'. But the reality is that the optic nerve and the light sensitive retina are a part of the anatomical and physiologic functional of the CNS, and that the picture presented to our mind (f of CNS) is-in fact-that image falling upon the retina. "There is a temptation to say that the eyes produce pictures in the brain." That "suggests the need of some kind of internal eye to see it-but this would need a further eye to see its pictures... and so on in an endless regress of eyes and pictures. This is absurd." (p. 7 Gregory)

What the eye sees is not an object, but a flat intangible image of the object. "We do not merely perceive our retinal image, we experience an external world of solid things." (p. 67 Blakemore). Visual perception is a model in brain hypothesis of the external world.

It would seem logical to suppose that there be an instantaneous feedback loop of information returning from the occipital cortex to the retina-to make corrections on that first instantaneous retinal image perception. The changing of focus of the lens of the eye being only the most obvious of at least several corrective influences upon that retinal image. Other corrective processes occurring mainly at the level of the retina.

The outside world makes its impression upon the retina as an image. There in the retina that image is processed for detail of color, shape, contrast, image edges, etc. Those instantaneous details in turn are transmitted as bits of information to the occipital cortex where the information is combined with and processed with information from one's other senses, and from memories to create our visual perception. But there is no secondary copy of the retinal image that passes beyond the retina nor deeper into the occipital or other neuronal substance of the central nervous system. Neither, of course, is there an 'inner-man', 'soul', or 'spirit' such as could, in turn, scrutinize any postulated such secondary picture of what is imaged on the retina. The notion of the deeper parts of the CNS and its mind as being able to observe some hypothetical secondary photograph is a myth. The solitary person, alone, uses the visual information to come to a creative grasp of the significance to him of what the retinal image means to him.

"Neurons present arguments to the brain based on the specific features they detect. Arguments on which the brain constructs its hypothesis and perception" of the individual's outer world in which he has his physical existence. (p. 91 Blakemore) "But the senses do not give us a picture of the world directly; rather they provide evidence for checking hypothesis about what lies before us." (p. 11 Gregory)

Does what one perceives require from him some immediate judgment or action... or not? The individual's moment-by-moment conscious awareness will have to decide. That consciousness being informed by one's visual and other senses, along with his recollections and knowledge from a life of past experience.

※　※　※　※　※

Phenomenology

Heaton wants to make it clear that "Phenomenology is not introspection." And so it seemed to me a good idea to make a little side trip into what is the nature of introspection, so that as I bumble along, I am at least clear on what Phenomenology is not.

In the process of introspection, we are said to be contemplating our private conceptual data which is being brought forth into our conscious awareness from our store of intangible imaginative memory. It is private data which we in the process of thought are attempting to organize into some particular thesis to satisfy some quest for our personal silent satisfaction or to be of some use to some project which we intend to utilize to some purpose in the tangible world of our bodily existence. It is thus shaped by thought into something of the nature of an idea which one intends to present in the course of one's conversation, perhaps. Or to expound in the writing of a letter or a paper to be read by some one or persons to some particular purpose.

As to the definition of Phenomenology, I come across four that we might consider.

1-to let that which shows itself be seen from itself.
OR 2-the intuitive appreciation of phenomena as they are immediately perceived.
Or 3-the study of the function of one's consciousness as experienced from a first-person's point of view.
OR 4-as Heaton puts it to us, "we actively grasp the meaning of experience as we live it."

I read through Husserl's little monograph of lectures which he originally delivered on the subject of Phenomenology. It was rather too theoretically complex for me to grasp. What Heaton has to say on the matter is a little more straightforward, especially in that he presents a couple of examples to give one some idea as to what he is talking about.

We are given now to understand that in the Phenomenology process the intent is to come suddenly into contact with, say, an object such as bouncing ball, or find oneself suddenly confronted with a situation as one is hiking into the countryside. In that suddenness, we make no conscious attempt to project into the encounter any preconceived idea of what it is that we have encountered. Instead, we just let the situation of the encounter express itself to us as we live with it in the moment. We live and are at one with it, and the object or the situation does and is capable of supplying to us through our senses, the nature of what it is. "We actively grasp the meaning of experience as we live it." "We do not split ourselves into an observer and an observed" (p. 298 Heaton) We are enabled thus to comprehend that by design and/or by its previously acquired habit, the mind becomes a part of our encounter with the object or situation and thus perceives its 'essence'. There **is an unspoken dialectic between the individual and** the object-or the situation. The mind overlooks and does not see the minutia and irrelevancies in the experience. The mind sees only the ball in its completeness and is aware of, but has disregarded the series of instant by instant images of the ball in its trajectory through time and space Aspects that cannot be merely glued together. But the mind is intuitively aware of the trajectory of the ball and has intuitively anticipated where the ball will be in its trajectory at the moment the person intends to grasp the ball in its flight. The mind adds an immediate short past and an immediate brief near future to what is perceives. Just so too, concerning a man who is involved with other persons in a square-dance. He lives the experience in its fullness and is at one with the other dancers and in the ritual of the performance. "The world as we know it is a construction to which the individual mind contributes as much by its molding forms as the object or situation contributes by its stimuli."

We perceive the top of the table as round, whereas our sensation is of an ellipse from the angle of our perspective. The object as it appears to us is a phenomenon or appearance perhaps very different from the external object before it came within the ken of our senses, says Durant in *The story of Philosophy*. (p. 297)

"In the spatial disorders occurring in lesions of the parietal lobes, the patient's body is locked in natural space. Thus he may be able to swat a fly which lands on his nose; but he is unable to point to his nose if asked to do so. The former action occurs purely in natural space, while the latter action requires an ability to abstract oneself from the here-and-now and to regard the body as an object in space." (p. 305 Heaton)

"We experience ourselves and others always as embodied selves, never as pure minds or subjects. Every emotion, thought, and perception involves a bodily experience." (p. 302 Heaton)

One language or two? "The toothache is essentially neutral. It may be described by the physicalist language of the body, and it may be denoted by the psychological or phenomenal 'language of mind'" The distinction between knowledge by description and knowledge by acquaintance. So, "the toothache may be classified under the captions both of Physical and Mental." "Neither language has philosophical priority, neither must be reduced to the other." "Reminiscent" and in agreement with "Spinoza's metaphysics of one reality with two attributes-extension and thought." (p 204 Abel)

"In straightforward visual experience, <u>objects disclose themselves</u> to us in the world immediately as objects. They directly engage and involve us and we are not aware of ourselves as subjects enclosed in our bodies separated from an independent external world." (p.298 Heaton)

This insight opens the relationship between what is seen and the act of seeing-to study. "We can now focus on how the world is constituted by us." Life is an experience that occurs in the world where it and its disorders can be studied. This insight is developed in <u>Phenomenology</u>, which is <u>the science of lived experience</u>. Dualism is rejected. The emphasis is on the unitary nature of man's behavior as a human being within and as a part of the world.

Light

Light has been one of the prime symbols of Deity, who is said to be the creator of the world. Yet He cannot be seen. As practically all light on this earth comes from the sun, the sun has been worshipped as though it were God.

"Light cannot be seen in itself. Space is dark, but light discloses itself by revealing objects and so creating the visual world. Lighting gathers together and organizes disparate objects so that a coherence is felt in the forms, colors, and significance of every scene." (p. 72 Heaton)

"In man's experience, in contrast to what can be deduced, everything is seen primarily in the space created by light. We are not ordinarily aware of looking at objects with our eyes. There is no feeling of separation between ourselves and the visual world." (p. 72 Heaton) "In the experience of visual perception we are unable to demarcate a perceiving subject from the object of perception, we are not aware of what is seen and who is seeing. We are at one with the world." (p. 86 Heaton)

"The realization that <u>vision is a dialectical process</u> between objects in the world and the person who sees them is the badly needed antidote to the nightmare of unbounded subjectivism and nihilism." (p. 86 Heaton)

＊　＊　＊　＊　＊

Concepts

"Concepts are tools of inference that can be carried over from the physical to the nonphysical realms." (p. 252 Pinker)

A typical person is said to possess perhaps not more than 10,000 concepts. The occipital cortex does not record a visual image or photographic representation of the visual image which falls upon the retina. Rather, it gathers bits of information which had first been dissected and processed in the retina. The details of that primary retinal data arrived as electrochemical bits of information to the primary layer of occipital cortex where it is further processed into separate details concerning color, primary features of the object of visual regard, (retinal image). The clues detected at synaptic level one (of the occipital visual cortex) are handed down for further processing to level two (of the occipital visual cortex), and this to level three, etc. Ever more deeply into the temporal area towards the hippocampus. At perhaps-say-level three or level four the data of the visual network has become aware of perhaps enough features such as to make one's consciousness aware of the outline of the face.

Further on down the chain of the neural net, sparsely scattered data of the several sensory systems is recombined into a particular concept such as a familiar face. The lowest neuronal layers of the deep temporal substance hand off that concept into the hippocampus where the concept is then bundled into a 'conceptual neuron', presented into conceptual form and processed (after much previous sorting) into first a short-term- and perhaps then to a long-term memory. Aspects of that concept are then redistributed abroad widely to the cerebral cortex by links which are subsequently available to the frontal lobes for subsequent retrieval as memory. By this time, the concept is represented by-say-20,000 separate neurons with each its own bit of information ready for retrieval as parts of a specific memory. Information of other cognitive aspects (smells, tastes, touch, auditory, etc.) of cognition being widely co-mingled with that from the visual input. Internal and external stimuli can again quickly access and re-assemble this information through interaction of conceptual cells of the hippocampus.

Should the conceptual mechanism in the posterior aspect of the hippocampus neuronal tissue be somehow destroyed, the cognitive aspect of one's precepts has no mechanism for creating any further long-term memory. Though whatever long-term memories previously produced are yet available for retrieval from some separate neuronal pathway (whence?) into the frontal lobe. In the sorting and culling process, much of the information that passed as bits into short term memory is destined to rattle about there briefly and then gradually fade into irretrievability. But the content of greatest relevance will have gained priority access to long-term memory processing which is concerned primarily with "getting the gist of" the concept. Having conceptually acquired the gist of a concept into long term memory, one then can easily enough fill-in the missing detail by imagination and confabulatory logic. But long term recollections too, undergo foreshortening-due to an enormous omission in the number of facts (as noted by William James).

✳   ✳   ✳   ✳   ✳

Visualizing

The memory and recollection of what the eye has seen is but the barely visualized faint negative of what the eye has once before seen. With many details ignored or filled in by one's imagination. Imagination itself being but another aspect of memory.

And we are aware that in states of toxicity from illness and substances one is capable of being very much deceived into believing that he is 'seeing' that which does not actually exist. And we are also much aware that the act of an intentional "recalling a past experience is a feat at which [something which] we oft must strain mightily. A feat which we often fail to bring off. "Often we do not know whether we have brought it off or not. So we may claim to have recalled something and yet may later be persuaded to withdraw the claim." (p. 278 Ryle)

The eye, produces the equivalent of a processed photograph such as that produced by a camera. The image on the retina is in fact directly perceived by the 'mind' as a function of CNS awareness and consciousness).

Interestingly, we are told that Descartes, working with an ox eye, cut away the sclera from the back of the eye. He was then astounded to note the image upon the ox retina of any object at which he pointed the ox eye.

As to the perception of the said retinal 'photograph' being a direct '*f* of CNS', leave us not make the mistake of supposing that that retinal image is _re_translated once more into a 'picture' for some intangible and unnecessarily postulated phantom-eye to some separate entity such as an intangible, 'spirit', or 'soul'.

And again, if there were this immortal 'inner-man' to see this image of a person that one were to picture (on an entirely inner stage of one's inner life?) how would it communicate the reality of its existence to you, who are supposedly housing both the private inner picture, and the intangible 'inner-man'. And what would be the physiological basis on which this intangible 'inner-man' functions. We are again faced with the problem of infinite regressions.

Consider here the concept of 'Occam's Razor'-the rule of parsimony. Preference for the simplest assumption that will fit the facts." (p. 31 Bateson) Rather than facilitate, this mistaken notion of an 'inner man' only complicates the already very real difficulty we experience in our effort to comprehend the mystery of vision.

Information from the eyes is indeed ordinarily transmitted to the occipital optical cortex of the CNS. We are left to understand that such information is then but sorted and processed so as to make the visual information meaningful and relevant to the CNS which does indeed thus utilize and deal with chemical-electric 'blips' to somehow produce to our awareness considerable information-though not an actual photographic image in the occipital cortex. Reminding us perhaps to be cognizant that the only actual image is located on the retina. "Though the processes of perception are not conscious, its products commonly do become conscious." (p. 142 Bateman) "The retina receives a lot of information that remains outside of consciousness." (p. 34 Bateman)

I have had the opportunity to examine and work briefly with a cortically blind patient. A helicopter blade had stuck the patient on the head, destroying his occipital cortex area. The peculiarity of this and other such cases is that they are apt to believe that they can yet see-though they are unable to demonstrate that. Though the eyes and the optic nerve still continue to function in the face of 'cortical blindness', the information has no alternative cortical area in which the information can be processed. It is thus the same thing 'as though' the eyes were blind-although in fact they be still functional. Function which then goes un-comprehended at or beyond the visual cortex. There are suggestions that perhaps a small secondary visual tract makes its way into the infra-tentorial area of the brain stem to dimly register there.

❋   ❋   ❋   ❋   ❋

Language Centers

There have been demonstrated to be particular areas of the cerebral cortex which pertain to language. Areas that in right handed persons are located in the left hemisphere.

Carl Wernicke, had a patient who could speak quite well, but was unable to understand the speech of others. An autopsy found the damaged cortex and he correctly hypothesized that this area was responsible for speech comprehension.

Wernicke's area is at the upper portion of the temporal lobe, just behind the auditory cortex, posterior to the left superior temporal gyrus and appears to be related to perception of language. Lesions in Wernicke's area usually produce a receptive aphasia-an inability to understand the speech of others. This though they themselves do not have an impairment in producing speech. When asked a question, they will respond with a sentence that is more or less grammatical, but which contains words that have little to do with the question or, for that matter, with each other. Strange, meaningless, but grammatical sentences come forth. Speech such as is described as a sort of word salad. This kind of aphasia is known as Wernicke's Aphasia, or receptive aphasia. It is not just about speech comprehension. People with Wernicke's Aphasia also have difficulty naming things, often responding with words that sound similar, or the names of related things, as if they are having a very hard time with their mental "dictionaries."

Broca's area is a language area in the left frontal cortex that appears to be related to the synthesis and motor aspect of the production of speech. It is involved in the motor production of language, as well as being vital in dealing with grammar itself. Damage to the area usually causes inability or difficulty in producing speech-expressive aphasia. But they usually have not much difficulty in understanding speech.

Paul Broca was a French neurologist who had a patient with severe language problems. Although the patient could understand the speech of others with little difficulty, the only word he could produce was "tan." Because of this, Broca gave the patient the pseudonym "Tan". After the patient died, Broca performed an autopsy, and discovered an area of the frontal lobe, just ahead of the motor cortex controlling the mouth, that had been seriously damaged. He correctly hypothesized that this area was responsible for speech production.

Physicians called the inability to speak aphasia, and the inability to produce speech was therefore called Broca's aphasia, or expressive aphasia. Someone with this kind of aphasia has little problem understanding speech. But when trying themselves to speak are capable only of slow, laborious, often slurred sequences of words.

They don't produce complete sentences, seldom use regular grammatical endings such as-ed for the past tense, and tend to leave out small grammatical words.

It turns out that Broca's area is not just a matter of getting language out in a motor sense, though. It seems to be more generally involved in the ability to deal with grammar itself, at least the more complex aspects of grammar. For example, when they hear sentences that are put into a passive form, they often misunderstand. If you say "the boy was slapped by the girl," they may understand you as communicating that the boy slapped the girl instead. (Blakemore)

Despite the fact that Broca's and Wernicke's Areas are in different lobes, they are actually quite near each other and intimately connected by a tract of nerves called the arcuate fascilicus-a white matter nerve tract. A lesion obstructing this tract produces what is called a conduction aphasia. They can understand speech, and they can (although with difficulty) produce coherent speech, but they cannot repeat words or sentences that they hear.

Reading and writing are a part of language as well, of course. But since these skills have only been around a few thousand years, they are not as clearly marked in terms of brain functioning as the basic comprehension and production areas.

The angular gyrus lies about halfway between Wernicke's area and the visual cortex of the occipital lobe. It seems to be implicated in in problems such as alexia (the inability to read), dyslexia (difficulties with reading), and agraphia (the inability to write.

In research involving the use of PET scans on people with these problems, the angular gyrus is not as active as it is in other people while engaged in reading or writing. However, problems such as dyslexia also can involve other areas of the brain, or not involve brain disorders at all

Nature of Nature

Mortal Monads

<u>We mere mortals</u> would needs must be thought of each as an embodiment of mind. **Monad** <u>in nature</u>. (No Cartesian duality) But a part of the physicality of each mortal being includes the physical substance of the CNS (brain), a function of which is what we call a rational and analytic 'mind'. A mortal 'mind' and rationality which though of physical origin, has a capacity to deal with the analysis of that which is merely intangibly conceptual and with ideas. Able to contemplate the underlying intangible 'mind' as the function of man's physical brain tissue. An ambiguous perspective that could conceivably underlie the nature of the universe in which we are imbedded. We needs must perceive of the limited reality of our 'mental' capacity when we consider that with the demise of individual man, there also does perish that part of him which we call by the name of 'mind' or 'f of CNS'. The Cartesian dualists do not concede to the perishability of the 'mind' of man-which they most prefer to call by the name of 'soul' or the 'spirit'.

✳   ✳   ✳   ✳   ✳

The Essential Question

Why is there something instead of nothing? I thought long and hard to come up with an answer to that. But why trouble you with that merely rhetorical device? It would be something like Rev. Wright had to say about the Obama rhetoric of 'Hope and Change'. "Just words. Just speeches." And yet my many scattered months of unplanned unemployment through the years (along with my share of life's other dilemmas and problems) has left me often philosophically inclined and with empty hours to ponder such riddles. The essence of it is this: there could not be a something unless there were a nothing to which one could compare it. Likewise, there could not be a nothing unless there were a something with which to compare it.

Are there parallel universes? (See recent Sc. Amer. articles on this exotic concept) They are only a theoretical consideration. The mathematics of it is beyond my poor powers of comprehension. I don't look for there ever to be any definitive evidence of the matter. Even to ask such a question gets one into difficulty with logic, for the singular word 'universe', to me, by definition denotes everything that exists.

The philosophical reality is that we individual mere mortals share in common the reality of the physical world in which we have our being, and which we must learn to navigate as best we can. And we may be well advised to deal meaningfully with one another throughout the course of our lives.

While on the other hand, we each have our individual mental 'being' and existence that goes on inside our individual round skulls. Each of us possesses our private life and private universe-as it were. Only in that sense then, perhaps, it might be said that there might appear to be 'parallel worlds'.

I occasionally close my eyes to one of those rare and blissful episodes of deep and dreamless sleep (like unto death). And from which I wake more than commonly refreshed. I am left to suppose that many of you have experienced that same sort of thing upon occasion.

I am left then to suppose that when at last I close mine eyes to that sleep eternal, the continuous chatter and motions of my mind shall cease, and from my private universe "earth's foundations shall depart and all you folks shall die"-(poem from Houseman). That all will cease to exist, and nothing more shall be, and time shall be no more.

✳   ✳   ✳   ✳   ✳

Appearance Versus Reality

It would seem that Descartes was confounded by yet another enigma (in addition to his misperception of the Cartesian mind/body 'dualism'). Namely that of <u>appearance versus reality</u> in the real physical world-of which we mortals are intimately a part. Perhaps that is <u>part of the explanation for Descartes' convenient retreat into the then prevailing concept of a God</u>. That retreat gave him the (at least temporary) bridge from his <u>presumption of a spiritual existence</u> in the mind of God-into the physical world of reality. And the confounding elusiveness of that reality versus the 'appearances' of reality. And for that matter, I see no practical difference whether we and the world exist together either rather within, or outside of the mind of God. For in either case it is mere speculation and provides us with no information as to the ultimate nature of God. A suggestion for our speculations and contemplation perhaps-but not evidence.

As to <u>that hint of a double entendre between the appearance and the reality behind that appearance</u>, there are few things more common to the experience of a human being. A problem with which we each have wrestled since birth. And we can well infer that our whole race of Homo sapiens has had to struggle with it since their very beginnings. Our experience of that continuing challenge, both as individuals and as a species, has and continues to keep us fully aware that we can not avoid the necessity of ongoing efforts to remain cognizant of that ever present discrepancy. The pragmatic aspects of our day-to-day existence requires us to make those distinctions in order to function with an improving efficiency. We might speak of that as being <u>the moral value of reality</u>. "The moral influence of nature upon every individual is that amount of truth which it illustrates to him." (Emerson)

Our very daily survival is dependent upon our continuing ability to distinguish between appearance and reality. To distinguish between a 'first impression' and a more considered later evaluation. We make those distinctions on the basis of our first-hand experience and at the cost of a certain price for each mistaken perception. Since our lives are short, our individual experience and judgment is necessarily always limited. In addition to our personal experience in the matter of perception of the reality behind appearances, we are culturally informed and guided by our family and tribe as a part of our education and upbringing. The learning process concerning this complex world and universe is a time consuming and difficult process that gives us pain and inconvenience. An inescapable reality of life. A process that is facilitated by engaging in the labor and difficulty of thought. What individual native wit and determination can we bring to that process?

> By education most have been misled;
> So they believe, because they were so bred.
> The priest continues what the nurse began,
> And thus the child imposes on the man.
> John Dryden

It is as though we mere mortals as a species were outcast naked and uninformed into this wide world and universe of infinite complexity. And left even to discover for ourselves that we do have some certain native and potential capacity to fend for ourselves and begin to comprehend the nature of the reality with which we are faced. Unless and until we take responsibility for our own intellectual progress, we remain ever the more hostage to **myth** and dogma.

✳ ✳ ✳ ✳ ✳

The Mind Of Nature
From Bateson's, *"Mind and Nature"*

The stated immediate task of his book was to construct a picture of how the world is joined together in its mental aspect. How do ideas, information, steps of logical or pragmatic consistency, and the like fit together? How is logic related to an outside world of things and creatures, parts and wholes? Darwin's *Origin of Species* in effect has not included 'mind' as an explanatory principle of life and evolution. But thought resembles evolution in being stochastic. That is to say, a sequence of events that combines a random component with a selective process so that only certain outcomes of the random are permitted to endure. Every step in evolution is an addition of information to an already existing system. (p.21 Bateson)

I am inclined to agree with those who suggest and suppose there to be a 'mind of nature'. [**Consider here the concept** of Marx's "Dialectical Materialism"] Does, perhaps, the mere mortal function of the 'mind' of each human-being parallel and mirror 'the-mind-of-mother-nature'. (in the brevity of each person's individual existences?)

Re: Marx's **Dialectical Materialism**;

Marx's materialism is based on 'Standing Hegel on his head', and transforming the Hegelian idealistic patter into a theory about the natural world. Instead of attributing the dialectical scheme to some Absolute or Objective Mind, <u>it is in Nature alone that the processes of overcoming contradictions takes place.</u>

Everything in the universe is interpreted as being the result of physical force in operation. But these forces, rather than operating merely in a mechanical manner, proceed in a dialectical fashion, achieving or evolving ever more; and more consistent and coherent features. The human world, which is, of course, the chief concern of the theory, represents a type of materialistic being, whose way of existence is determined by the material factors involved in his attempts to produce sufficient material goods for his survival. (p 91 Popkin)

"The great basic thought which dialectical materialism inherited from Hegel was that that world is not to be comprehended as a complex of ready made things, but as a complex of processes." (p.6 Abel)

"A poem is never finished, it is only abandoned." Neither is a life ever completed to fulfillment-it only comes unfinished to its demise.

✳   ✳   ✳   ✳   ✳

"There is little doubt that the evolution of intelligence has involved a gradually increasing power of prediction." The chief "value of remembering is not primarily that it allows one to reminisce about the past, but that it permits one to calculate coldly about the unknown future." Subsequently, the "sharing of learned ideas by social animals has added an entirely new dimension to the progress of evolution." This, noted especially in primates (and especially in mathematics and sciences) allows the experience of the individual human being to become reflected in the behavior of other members of the same social group-even into subsequent generations. (p. 115 Blakemore)

"The emergence of a kind of communal intellect-'the collective mind' of man-pushes forward his biological progress at a prodigious rate." In 1953 some scientists were tossing sweet potatoes onto a sandy beach for a group of macaque monkeys. One of the monkeys discovered how to get rid of the unpalatable sand by washing the sweet potato in a nearby creek. Within a year 90% of the monkeys of that troop were following her example. And when grain was scattered onto the sandy beach, that same monkey soon figured out that by throwing the material onto the seawater it became palatable. For the sand sank to the bottom leaving her to harvest the purified grain at the surface. Most of the group soon followed that same procedure. 'The collective mind' at work. (pp. 116-117 Blakemore)

Language even then further facilitates the evolution of the communal mind. But such methods of transfer are subject to the possibility of progressive distortion, like that which characterizes the spreading of a rumor. And hence all the conditions will exist for a kind of evolution of ideas. (p. 117, Blakemore)

There have been experiments in which baby chimps have been raised side-by-side with human babies. "The chimps proved more than a match for their human infant companions in both agility and intellect until the baby 'naked apes' began to speak. Then, apparently repeating the evolutionary history of man, the human infants soon outstripped their Simian colleagues." The chimp, lacking speech, falls behind the human infant. (p. 124 Blakemore)

❋   ❋   ❋   ❋   ❋

Theory Of Time
according to George Ellis
Meralo, Zeeya; "Tomorrow Never Was"; Discover Magazine; June, 2015 pp.39-45.
-Abstract by RGB-

Einstein's view concerning time is that time is an illusion. Says he, "people like us who believe in physics, know that the distinction between past, present, and future is only a stubbornly persistent illusion." He "replaced the Newtonian standard Universal time with a discordant, relative view in which different people would disagree about the duration of events and even the order in which they occurred." These differences in view being, for example, as of the nature of whether the moon seems to be rising to the left or to the right of a particular church steeple-depending upon one observer being stationed more to the north, compared to the other stationed more to the south.

Einstein's view was that of "a block universe" where the past, present, and future were all simultaneously one whole and complete construct. A universe in which one person perceives as future, that which is perceived by someone else as a past. Depending upon one's position and motion. The future, though remaining unknown to me, could seem to another as being already written. A universe devoid of uncertainty and exclusive of probability-at which he scoffed, saying, "God does not play dice." A universe in which the 'forward' aspect of time is considered to be arbitrary.

While George Ellis had a great respect for the work and concepts of Einstein, he began to postulate that Einstein went too far. Ellis, proposing rather, that the future is not set nor predetermined. If all is predetermined as Einstein's 'block universe' would suggest, then the likes of Hitler and us other miscreants would have had no choice in the error of their ways. Ellis suggests that view as being dangerous, because it robs us of free-will and moral responsibility. He wants to put time back into physics, allowing the cosmos to create fate, and giving us the ability to change our destiny. He is wont to suggest that though the past and present are fixed and determined, the future remains a collection of possibilities and uncertainties until it merges into the present.

The concept of Ellis is that the <u>leading edge of space-time marks the present</u>, as it moves outward moment-by-moment, transforming tomorrow's maybes into yesterday's fixed happenings.

Einstein could not come to terms with the then evolving Quantum Mechanics. A view which dealt with and focused on small-scale details of reality and which dealt specifically with uncertainty and probability. On the other hand, these more recent suggestions of Ellis do and are able to come to terms with Quantum Physics. Physicists have known for decades that Quantum Mechanics and general relativity are incompatible. Their "notions of the nature of time has been one of the major obstacles in uniting the two frameworks into a single theory."

Ellis proposes that at the leading edge of the evolving 'block universe', the future crystallizes into the past through a sequence of microscopic quantum events. At each event, particles are forced to transform from their original uncertain quantum states-where they juggle conflicting identities-and settle into one rigid identity. As adjacent particles go through this process, a wave of certainty converts the open future into the closed past."

Ellis maintains that this quantum collapse is happening everywhere about us. For example, each time a quantum of light is absorbed by a living trees, quantum uncertainty changes into certain.

❋ ❋ ❋ ❋ ❋

To mortal man time and motion is perceived <u>subjectively</u> as the before-and-after in the memory of our couscous minds. Time and motion appear to march in lock-step, and forever only in a forward direction. We consciously deal with time's irrevocable mandates in the execution of our daily lives. Without that motion and the time by which we measure distance, even our clocks would be of no use to us, and our lives would be akin merely to still-life painting upon a wall.

But we also become aware of an <u>objective</u> aspect of time in our awareness of the changing of seasons through the years, and the metamorphosing of insects and our own immediate families. Infants gradually cease to be infants, and eventually take leave of the home in which they once dwelled.

Little Things
Little drops of water,
Little grains of sand,
Make the mighty ocean
And the pleasant land.
So the little moments,
Humble though they be,
Make the mighty ages
Of Eternity.
Julia Fletcher

We find considerable utility in the process of logic, but also become aware that our logic not infrequently fails to arrive us at valid sums and conclusions. Hence we retain always a healthy skepticism concerning even our own conclusions, and retain a healthy compulsion to reexamine those calculation. We are often at odds with the conclusions of others. We remain generally good natured and sometimes even amused by such as the conclusions of a Philosopher such as Berkeley whose misleading postulations we can admire for their cleverness, even in our distrust in them. There seems little cause for one to be vexed at him, since his pleasantly humorous conclusions are of not significant consequence to us.

And so, though I do not look forward to what is commonly the uncomfortable process of dying, I have no objection to what I suppose and am hopeful will be the blessed 'sleep eternal'. An end to incessant external and internal wrangling and discontent. An end to vain hope, disappointment, and the troubles and difficulty of sustaining a somewhat pointless, useless, and insignificant life. I can't imagine why I would object never to have been born in the first place. "Common sense tells us our existence is but a brief crack of light between two eternities of darkness" (Vladimir Nabokov)

❊　❊　❊　❊　❊

We note "the wisdom of the body being matched by its stupidities." (p.141 Abel) Through metabolism one's body is generated and evolves. One remakes one's body by absorption and ingestion of plant and animal life. The cells of one's body are almost all replaced perhaps every seven to ten years. Who then am I? What is the continuity? "To ask whether the body is the object of experience or the source of experience is to forget that the process of becoming a person rests on both modes." (p. 195 Abel)

"Our thoughts and intentions emerge from background causes of which we are often unaware; and over which we exert no conscious control." (says Sam Harris-neuroscientist-in his book, *Free Will*.) We do not have the freedom we think we have. But, (says Michael Shermer) "if we define free will as the power to do otherwise, the choice to veto one impulse over another is free will." (p. 15 Sc. Amer. August 2012) [see page 51]

"To live is to feel ourselves fatally obliged to exercise our liberty to decide what we are going to do and what we are going to be in this world. Even when in desperation we abandon ourselves to whatever may happen, we have decided not to decide."

❊　❊　❊　❊　❊

Freudianism Returns

Beginnings of Psychology

When the field of Psychology had its beginnings some 200 or 300 years ago it was thought its practitioners would find a key to study human beings in a completely different way. With data that was not then (or now) available to teachers, detectives, biographers, etc. Hidden data which could not be represented on the stage or in the pages of the novel. (Such data as were thought to be isolated into obscure nooks of the CNS in which the ghostly 'inner persons' dwelt.) Yes, Psychology aspired for a key and direct access to the 'inner residents' themselves (that supposed 'inner-man' of Descartes' conception). What inner residents would these be?-reference again to the independent immortal 'soul' of Dualism.

The visible deeds and audible words of real persons were thought themselves not to be expressions of the quality of character or intellect. But thought only to be external symptoms or expressions of their private hidden 'souls'. Proposing that the mind (by which they meant this hidden 'soul') is its own place and that in that inner life, "each of us lives a life of a ghostly Robinson Crusoe." "But the mind is not in place, either physically or metaphorically." It is a function-of the cerebral cortex. (p. 12 Ryle)

That is the difficulty of the concept of 'the inner man' or 'soul'. What could possibly connect the intangible to the physiology of the tangible body? A difficulty that eventually suggests to us, the concept of 'mind' as being a function of the CNS. And the motivating initiation of acts, of thought, and behavior, as being not will or volition, but rather, a combination of a mortal being's predispositions, acquired habits, acquired knowledge and information.

And so Psychology has had to give up the idea that it is about this something (soul) that the other human studies were not about. The study of Psychology too, is left in the pursuit of its goals with only the same data which has always been available to playwrights, models, and teachers: namely, the visible deeds and audible words of mortal beings. Spoken and unspoken utterances, tones of voice, facial expressions, and gestures.

When we are unable to explain the cause of action or behavior, that question is a psychological one. Once we have insight into that cause, it often turns out that the explanation is economic, physiologic, physical, social, etc.

Psychology must then conciliate and come to deal with physiological information they can gather via the reactions and verbalizations of normal, abnormal, and pathological statistical states available to them from specimens of the spectrum of existential human beings. The spectrum of variation of we who constitute mankind. Dealing with every-day neuro-physiology and using what tools are available to them for use in experimentation. Examining alterations of human behavior as caused by neuro-degenerative disease, medications, and CNS states of toxicity. The testing of cognition, and responses to variations. And the variations among we mortals are manifold.

✻   ✻   ✻   ✻   ✻

The Talking Cure

Eric Kendall is among the world's leading experts on learning and memory. He tells us, "you can't have a meaningful science of brain without having a meaningful science of the 'mind'. "Flawed as it may be, Freud's is still a coherent and intellectually satisfying view of the mind." (p. 60 McGowan)

Thus now the attempt "to put the study of 'mind' back into the study of the brain." (p. 58 McGowan)

Neuroscience was in its infancy in the 1890s. A science in avoidance of subjective experience in its quest. The quest to determine "how does the actual stuff of being a person relate to the tissues, physiology, and anatomy of the brain?" "How is it that dreams, fantasies, memories, and feelings (as subject matter of cells) emerge from a piece of flesh?" Little was known of it. (p. 56 McGowan)

Neuroscience methods of research were primitive and so unpromising that Freud gave up his attempt at any objective study of the mind and propounded his own evolving theory of mind. As in its inception, Freudian theory still believes in and stresses that subjective experiences are meaningful and important in the function of the 'mind'. And what "Freud wrote about" are the things that "every waking person thinks about." Psychoanalysis "has a much richer tapestry of both words and concepts than Neuro-biology." (p. 60 McGowan)

Freud conceived the mind as constantly generating powerful wishes, fears, and desires. And inherently conflicted between unconscious impulses and inhibitory mechanisms (i.e. Id, Ego, and Superego). Subjective modes like pleasure and rewards seem to "arise from events in the limbic system of the brain, a center of emotion loosely parallel to Id: while the prefrontal cortex handles self-control and the oversight of habitual responses (sort of like an Ego)." (p. 60 McGowan)

Psycho-analytic theory suggests that the newborn child is something akin to a savage barbarian. Our minds come to be divided. The primal drives of the subconscious rage beneath its surface and are said to generate uncouth lust, aggressions, fantasies, and wishes that come to be repressed by internal sensors. "Ego (reason) struggles to contain this mad turmoil", producing a constant contest in our ever wandering mental processes. It is suggested that most of what we do and think is shaped by subconscious impulses unrecognized to ourselves.

If the impulses are as the wind in the sails, reason and character might be said to act as the rudder that gives direction and destination to the hope.

> And every mind decideth,
> The way that he shall go.
> . . . .
> 'Tis the set of the sails
> And not the gales,
> That tells the way we go.
> . . . . . .
> 'Tis the set of the soul,
> That determines the goal,
> And not the calm or the strife.
> Ella Wheeler Wilcox

✳   ✳   ✳   ✳   ✳

The internal struggle for one's self-control predisposes to anxiety-depression and pervasive misery. "Psychoanalysis is about having someone help you face facts that you would rather not face up to." (p. 58 McGowan) It is intended to translate into a deepening self-knowledge. The big picture then and now is that the 'mind' is at war with itself. (p. 60 McGowan)

Introspection is supposedly a species of perception. But one which is probably more retrospective, especially if connected to some one of the many inner agitations to which we mere mortals are so commonly predisposed.

Introspection however is not fully reliable. Intelligence, volition, ambition, belief, etc. are now better understood, not as mental entities, but as dispositions to behave in certain ways. Their significance is as much public and social as private. In Freud's concept of the unconscious, we are seldom aware of all our own basic drives, impulses, and motives. Only the tip of the iceberg of our subconscious is visible to ourselves.

For the Ego to 'rationalize' is somewhat the opposite of what it is 'to reason'. A pretense to one's self. And tends to reduce the stature and trustworthiness of our state of intuition. Yes, always some tendency for reason to become servant to passion as self-interest spills over into greed. People tend to paint a halo of logic over their misconduct by providing various plausible explanatory derivations to conceal their underlying motifs and conduct.

This business of rationalizing becomes upon analysis, rather hazy as a valid distinctive attribute of mind. In a person with strong moral character, the Superego remains yet a force to counter this 'rationalizing' misbehavior of the Ego. And beyond that, the unwritten 'mores' of society also contribute to keeping the Ego agenda an honest participant.

Always, within the psyche remains the subconscious contest of the mind at war with itself. Reason and the Superego pitted against the Id and the rationalizing pretext. The mind forever at war with itself to some degree, striking a balance of self-censorship and raw self-interest in the living of a life within the world, and with all of those about him. One is nudged and imposed upon to maintain an acceptable deportment- lest one find himself unpleasantly disciplined and more sternly imposed upon by the world and society of which he is a part.

But in addition to that, the individual must also continuously struggle with himself concerning his inner solitary being. Self accusation and guilt-account of being invested both in one's Id and Superego are forever at odds within oneself.

One has always 'the heavy bear' agenda (Id), yet is inevitably required to submit to various agendas within society and those always several agendas at cross purposes to one another within himself. Inescapably, one's physiologic and psychic needs keep one subjected to the judgmental and punitive aspects of one's society. And one remains always a double agent within oneself. One needs always to grasp for a sense of stability and security within himself and within society.

❊　❊　❊　❊　❊

Treating Brain Damage

Dr. Solm was "treating patients with strokes and brain injury as a neurobiologist." (p. 57 McGowan)

But in his study of Philosophy he was "hearing about dreams, wishes, sex, and fantasy." In his inquiring as to as to where these things were being studied in his profession he discovered that nobody was engaged in that pursuit. Previously it was thought that "brain-damaged people didn't need psychiatric help because their problem was that of a 'broken-brain'." (p. 58 McGowan)

Psychoanalytic ideas were still providing treatment for mental illness, but scientists in Neurobiology rejected Psychoanalysis. There seemed at that time to be no objective evidence to show that psychoanalysis made any sense in the face of the damaged brain.

Neuro-imaging since the 1990s has at last given some objective markings of mental events (however yet crude these markings be). Many brain researchers have believed that only cognition and behavior have been well-suited for study. They considered that "emotions were to be dismissed as detritus." (p. 59 McGowan)

"Though still treating strokes and brain injury as a neurobiologist Solms now began to take training in Psychoanalysis." (p. 57 McGowan) Now that modern research tools were becoming available to such pursuits, he began to approach their problems with Psychoanalysis and evaluating their deep strange delusions and hallucinations. He tells us that "someone whose brain and life have been shattered clearly needs counseling as well as medical treatment." (p. 58 McGowan)

> The brain within its groove
> Runs evenly and true;
> But let a splinter swerve,
> 'twere easier for you

To put the water back
When floods have slit the hills,
And scooped a turnpike for themselves,
And blotted out the mills.
Emile Dickinson

We mortals often prefer to see the world as we wish it were. Facing the facts is difficult, requiring sustained mental labor and a high functioning brain. It became now much more clear to Solms just how difficult it was for them-the brain damaged (for anyone-actually) to face the troublesome facts of their lives. "Damaged brains are less up to the task and are beset with considerable confusion." A bewildered patient is inclined to retreat into a confabulation amnesia. In consequence, these patients end up living predominantly in their private fantasy world. A confabulatory imaginary living-out of their fantasies. One must presume that these tendencies are fundamental and much the same-to a lesser degree-in non-injured brain situations as well. (p. 58 McGowan)

"Freud had put the subconscious on the throne of the kingdom of the mind." (p. 60 McGowan) Finally, in the 1980s some studies began to support the idea. Recent studies indicate that as suspected, "people process most information (especially social data like other people's behavior) in the subconscious mind." (p. 60 McGowan)

It seems in fact, that we tend to "make decisions often without much input from conscious thought. Some unconscious part of the brain decides well before the conscious mind does so." It now appears that Freud seems to have been correct in postulating unconscious thought to be at the center of psychology. If anything, it begins to appear that he may have been under-estimated.

* * * * *

Interestingly, I notice on TV in a program, "Breakthrough", that consciousness is experimentally suspended when a micro-voltage of electricity is applied to a specific site in the hippocampus. And immediately upon discontinuation of the electro stimulation, the interrupted state of consciousness returns to where it was paused.

And in that same program there is this concerning the matter of decision making. It is noted that an encephalogram demonstrates that the moment a person decides consciously to act is preceded (by about seven seconds) by a subconscious burst of activity of which the person is <u>not</u> consciously aware. That subconscious electric signal predicts that the person is going to act. There is then this question: if one's actions are actually initiated in the subconscious, how can one be said to be responsible for one's own actions? Exculpation? And yet, pushing the experiment one step further, the electrical pattern demonstrates that just before the lapse of that seven second interval, one can consciously inhibit the anticipated act and its electrical signal.

Tim Wilson (University of Virginia) seems to suggest another aspect of "the nature of unconscious thought that emerges" as being "radically different" from that of the Freudian view." To him, subconscious thought begins to look like "a fast, efficient way to process large volumes of data" rather than just entirely a conceptual area of impulses and fantasies. (p. 60 McGowan)

Still, it cannot be said that at least some remnant of 'the heavy bear' does not still reside within the subconscious. It might be suggested that some taming of 'the heavy bear' occurs also at the subconscious as well as at the conscious level of one's psyche.

Motivations like pleasure and reward seem to arise from the limbic emotional system, roughly parallel to "Id". The "prefrontal cortex seems to handle self-control and acts as an over-ride upon habitual responses." A book by Damasio and Pinesap (*The Emotional Brain*) concludes "that emotions are not irrational intrusions into reason, but rather, are intimate to rational thought." (p. 59 McGowan)

Emotions show up in various species, ranging from chickens to people. Note the attachment of mother to child, and child to mother. When that attachment is broken it leads to a depressive state (in both). Possibly some survival value in that.

The evolving of Neuro-psychoanalysis seems also to be on the verge of resolving other psychiatric conundrums.

Internal Dialog

The combining now of both subjective and objective information begins to show evidence of a 'Default Mode Mechanism' that keeps the mind much preoccupied with electrical chatter, and daily utilizing 80% of the brain's energy consumption. But what is its purpose? Beneath the surface of consciousness "our minds continuously sift through thoughts about ourselves and our experiences." This network of neural regions is active during mind wandering, daydreaming, free association, and other dreamy introspective states. The very business that not infrequently interferes with our inability to get to sleep. We tend to reminisce over memories and feelings. We dream up fears and fantasies of the future that generate the raw material that the 'talking cure' taps into. The internal dialog seems to run continuously according to McGowan.

Having then freed ourselves of the notion that there is a second entity (besides the tangible organic brain or CNS) inside each human skull, we then might consider what is the origin or cause of any bodily action and human behavior. And what it is that brings forth human intelligence? What is the explanation as to why we mere mortals seem predisposed to gather knowledge, experience, skills, and sometimes even some little valid judgment and wisdom? It would seem to be a mandate from within our genes ((instinct) to pursue these elusive quests, just as it is a genetic trait of wolves, bears, lions etc. to pursue any sort of fleeing game. And just as also it is the propensity for creatures of prey to flee the predator.

We human beings come progressively to facilitate our passage through the difficulties, dilemmas, and dangers of this harsh competitive world on the basis of analytical thought and reason. This business seems to have proven itself a useful strategy. A herd instinct among us, conjoined with a gift for generating analytical thought, and supplemented by intercommunication with language has produced an evolving culture and inventive civilizations that reshape the very surface of a planet such as to enable us to live in ever greater comfort and pursue our individual destinies and personal objectives. But still, we have created no successful utopia, "and man's inhumanity to man makes countless thousands mourn." And our residual ignorance of the nature and workings of the world, universe, and ourselves remains yet far beyond our poor powers of comprehension. The territories of the human brain, mind, and of Philosophy are yet by me to be more tentatively reconnoitered.

Conceptual Expansion

Default Mode

The combining now of both subjective and objective information begins to show evidence of a 'Default Mode Mechanism' that keeps the mind much preoccupied with electrical chatter, and daily utilizing 80% of the brain's energy consumption. A network of neural regions seems to be active during mind wandering, daydreaming, free association, and other dreamy introspective states. But what is its purpose? The volcanic subconscious seems as if continuously to toss up fragments of scenarios, loose memories, and unwanted worries into our conscious awareness, to tempt us into thoughtful consideration and ponderings. The very business that not infrequently interferes with our ability to get to sleep, or burden the mind with vague anxieties.

Neural Networks

For a more scientific conception of the nature of human consciousness, let us then switch from what we know to be the functional units of our brain (i.e. neurons), to a conceptual theory of 'neural networks'. A higher order of understanding.

Consciousness would appear to have as its underpinning a rather large system of 'neural networks' into which it is fed by neurological connections from outlying areas of the various five sensory systems. And simultaneously from the internal bodily perceptual state of one's being as continuously monitored and edited by memory and conceptual networks.

The networks feed into a sort of 'cloud' of our unified CNS functional state which we are want to designate as man's 'intangible mind'. The notion of networks begins to lift us a notch closer in transcendence to an understanding of the immaterial realm of conceptual being.

✳   ✳   ✳   ✳   ✳

Expansion Of Consciousness

Consciousness changes from infancy into adulthood. Along with the expansion of the content of one's cognitive mind (f of CNS) and memory, we think of 'the mind's' existence more in connection with adults, than in children.

In childhood and early teens we are evolving our powers of reason, our morals, 'character', and individual personhood. Our organized memories do not take us back beyond the time in our lives when we first begin to organize those memories out of the chaos of mere vague perceptive impressions. Perhaps we have but only a few vague memories that date as far back to, say, three or four years of age?

Early to late teens we seem to be evolving Ego, sense of individuality, and self-sufficiency. And displaying our capacity for an ability to develop skills and produce services that in later years we were capable of harnessing for use as a source of our economic sustenance. And acquiring some social graces to prepare us for some facility in navigating through the social aspects of customary civil adult society.

As adults we begin to recognize more fully that "we too, the beaten path must tread, on which our sires of yore have lead". In later adulthood we most have gradually come to see ourselves as work-a-day 'responsible' citizens.

In our early declining adulthood we begin to think of ourselves somewhat more as a conscious rational mind and begin to recognize our physical being as of the nature of a slowly declining physical transportation system and a servant of our needs, wishes, and intentions.

In old age we tend to become more preoccupied in recollections of our own past, in the consequences of our past and current policy, and speculation into the physical-psychological aspects of being.

Among the various 'omnis' which theologians are want to postulate as an attribute to a God, one might also suggest omni-focus of conscious attention. One might postulate that a Deity would focus and be aware of the totality of that-which-is: and what is continuously evolving and occurring at all times. But we mere mortals are capable or only a mere minuscule of any such awareness of that. In one's waking-state, with eyes wide open, visual perceptions continuously stream into ones CNS as do auditory perceptions from one's ears. But for us (as mere mortals) these are little more than a plethora of insignificant background chatter- unless or until we have cause to focus our conscious attention to some small but significant proportion of that input which we suppose to be relevant to our private well-being of the moment-or of leisurely interest.

Natural Ethics

There would appear to be an **ethic in all of human affairs**. "Moral reasoning is not a cultural artifact invented for convenience and it is and always has been a vital glue of society. The means by which transactions are made and honored to ensure survival. Every society is guided by an ethical presence [customs, mores, and laws] and every one of its members is expected to follow moral leadership and ethics-based tribal law. Evidence exists of an instinct to behave ethically, or at least to insist on ethical behavior in others." Psychologists, for example, point out a seemingly universal propensity among mankind and other animals to detect cheaters and to respond to them with intense moral outrage.

"People by and large have a certain capacity for spotting deception in others, and are equally clever in constructing deceptions of their own." We are regularly exposed and involve ourselves in self-righteous gossip. This even while we long for sincerity in all our relationships. "Even the tyrant is sterling in prose, invoking patriotism and economic necessity to justify his misdeeds. And environmentalists inevitably carry the game too far, using it as an instrument for gaining political power. That broad and mostly hidden agenda comes from the left, usually the far left. How to get power? is what they have in mind. The aim is to expand governmental power." "Relax your guard when these people are in power and your property rights go down the tube." (pp. 151-153 Wilson)

"Each of us finds a comfortable position somewhere along the continuum that ranges from complete with-drawl and self-absorption on the one hand, to full civic engagement and reciprocity at the other. The position is never fixed. We fret, vacillate, and steer our lives through the riptide of countervailing instincts that press from both ends of the continuum" (ambiguities and dilemma). "Our lives are therefore an insoluble problem, a dynamic process in search of an indefinable goal." These lives are a predicament. The nature of our species is to make moral choices and seek fulfillment in a changing world by any means it can devise. The great majority of the 7 billion people who fill this world are very poor. One billion exist on the edge of starvation. All struggling to raise the quality of their lives any way they can. (ibid. page XX1)

Though we do discover the motives of persons, the process of discovering them is not immune from error. But nor are the errors impossible of correction. The way a person discovers his own long-term motives is much the same in which he discovers the motives of others. On the other hand, one's insight into his own inclinations are not apt to be unbiased. An impartial and discerning spectator is often a better judge than ourselves of one's own inclinations and motives. We see that to be contrary to the theory that holds that each person possesses privileged access to the well-springs of his own actions.

Spirituality and Consciousness

By the time one's children depart the nest in the waning of one's middle years of life, a parent is commonly apt to be in the process of re-evaluating the structure of his personal life (see *"Aims and Objectives"* by C.N.Parkinson). By degree, one tends to sink more deeply into introspection with the passing of years. The moments of leisure are less focused on the here-and-now and one spends more time rummaging through the old memory banks, and wondering what might have been, and comparing that with the more unsatisfactory aspects of the past and present. [see Whitman's poem, *Maude Miller*: "Of all sad words of tongue or pen, the saddest are these, 'it might have been...'"]

In the late middle years of adulthood one's frame may still be periodically racked with hormonal surges even while he may begin to wrestle with the possibility of improving his vague stature of honorable character and personhood as it might appear to the minds of those who occupy one's circle of acquaintances: and considering the image of his stature into posterity. <u>Individual personhood</u>-the symbolic life. On the one hand man is irrevocably destined to succumb to the divine fires of passion: while on the other hand, he tries to master, organize, and constrain his passions to some degree. A man generally aspires to be more than just a work-a-day breadwinner and handy man. A woman most commonly aspires to be more of a model of radiant motherhood, than merely a lusty toss-in-the-hay and a good cook. Vague aspiration always of 'persona', 'face', and stature-of-being.

There seems <u>not</u> a great deal of natural preoccupation of the pre-pubescent individual with sexuality despite a culturally imposed awareness of that sexuality. But about the time of puberty, there evolves the hormonally induced cultural preoccupation with thoughts, desires, and vague intentions of sexual acting-out. And along with that, a dawning instinct for bravado, independence of mind, and interest in the pursuit of other physically satisfying activity. All of which are present in the background preparation for the appropriate adult sex role to serve the individual when one matures to the adult physiologic hormonal status. And into adulthood, "there is nothing in human affairs so characteristic as the readiness of men, this side of senility, to pursue women-unless it be the readiness of women this side of the grave, to be pursued." (p. 100 Durant)

It is the case however that in recent decades, our society increasingly confronts the adolescent with rather an overburden of explicit sexual material which undoubtedly causes him unnecessary confusion and embarrassment; and probably predisposes to a somewhat higher incidence of neurosis and personality disorders in our 'civilized' populations.

✳ ✳ ✳ ✳ ✳

Speculative Philosophy

Would there exist anything at all if there were no creatures with sensory systems to perceive its manifestations? If a tree in some remote forest falls unseen and unheard, can it be said to make a noise?

Here we encounter Berkeley's monism explanation in which he posits that you and I and all that exists in the world and universe are all nothing more than ideas in the mind of God. A clever hypothesis for dealing with the slippery aspects of Philosophy, though merely a rhetorical gimmick. But it makes little difference whether we are each but an idea in the mind of God, or if our waking state is just a dream (our dreams then being only sub-dreams). For, pragmatically, our situation is unchanged and the dilemmas we face in this world and universe persist unto us unchanged, whether Berkeley be right or wrong.

The following verse by Ronald Knox, pertaining to Berkeley's Philosophic non-materialistic conception of the world and universe:

A young man suggested that God must be aware and find it strange that a tree on the 'quad' seemingly continued to exist even when there was nobody on the quad to have it in his perception. The second verse of the poem responded to the first verse as follows:

Your astonishment's odd.
I am always about in the quad.
And that's why the tree
Will continue to be,
Since observed by-
> Yours faithfully
> GOD (Berkeley's notion of)

❇   ❇   ❇   ❇   ❇

We are told that Berkeley and Hume did put their trust in sensory experience as a reliable source of knowledge. For to explain through observation and gain knowledge by inductive inference must be the only means by which we can discover truth.

Berkeley still had some reservations and said something to the effect, "when we put our hands near a fire we feel pain; when we put sugar in our mouth we experience pleasure." "Then, why should one think that any of our other sensations of shape and color, or of loudness and tone, originate in the material properties of objects"? (pp. 75-76 Blakemore)

It appears here that they are playing word games with us. For fire does contain heat (which-in excess and in contact with us-we then interpret as pain). And the taste of sugar is perceived as the quality of sweetness-a quality which we do perceive as pleasant-as well as sweet.

Which is presumably also why a tree which falls unseen and unheard by mortal being in an unpopulated area of our world can be supposed also to make a noise when it crashes to the ground.

Creatures with minds to attend and focus, do ponder the meaning of various and many physical manifestations. Those pondered perceptions are an un-distilled 'information' and a 'knowledge' of sorts. Information and knowledge ever in need of refinement and expansion.

Each individual being is an active force within the universe as well as inevitably acted upon. Reciprocity-seemingly one of the underlying principles of the Universe.

We mortals each absorb, possess, and share a small portion of the total intellect and knowledge (and superstitious tendencies) of the species. We have each but a tiny duration of existence in which to perceive, ponder, and contribute our speculative notions of the nature of reality to an accumulating tome or encyclopedia of sorted, organized, and distilled (and hopefully valid) information.

The reality in which we are imbedded certainly has a long history far beyond my brief 80 years. Through 20 or 30 recent centuries only a small portion of that history has come down to us from various and contradictory oral and written sources. The further back we look, the more vague and uncertain is that history. Additional data from prehistory also trickles down to us from our studies of Paleontology, Archeology and Geology. And Astronomy gives us glimpses of data from long past ages and eons of time. But as to the beginnings of 'that-which-is'-that is even more highly speculative. Suggested origins from either a big bang or an eternal Deity are no more informative than, "its turtles all the way down". One needs must again come to the conclusion that there is perhaps a great much that is unknown, and some of which is probably also unknowable to we mere mortals. What after all is there for one yet then to know other than that which is unknown-and perhaps unknowable?

How does that which is the <u>immaterial</u> of one's consciousness and the 'mind' come to be <u>derived from</u> the <u>material reality</u> of the living tissues of mortal man's CNS? One could as well suggest that the material universe is derived from an eternity of immaterial stuff. It could well be the case.

There are lessons one might note from Paleontology: the high antiquity of man, the law of progress of humanity, a linear as well a parallel development of creatures....

As to the WHY of the existence of a physical world and universe in which we have our existence, and the WHY of one's own existence, we must consider that reality to be based upon POSSIBILITY, combined with an element or PROBABILITY. A possibility and probability that we know to exist because it does exist in at least one's own being. Another possibility would be that there is a-nothing that exists, but we have only speculative access as to that. As to my own individual existence, it too needs must have sprung from what was only a possibility, which was based upon (among a host of other possibilities) the pre-existence of my own two parents. And I was only one of nine of what were many possibilities of that marriage. We can easily suppose that there were many other possibilities of their union that failed to materialize- three that we know of. An indirect evidence that not all possibilities are inevitably realized. If it were otherwise, they would be known as certainties.

There would seem to be a difference between actual vs. speculative possibilities. For, as we conceptually imagine of possibilities, we find that when we strive with methods and materials at hand to "invent them" into the real world, the most of them end up being 'stillborn', i.e. nonfunctional. Just a mass of material that does not evolve into any functional utility. And yet, some of which can be tweaked into functionality by imaginative thought and experimentation. Only some few of those imaginary possibilities prove to be viable in the tangible world of reality. Another matter that seems to cast doubt on such speculative possibilities as 'Multiverses' (as opposed to Universe) and 'string theory' in the field of Physics.

A few hundred years ago Newton conceived and mathematically supported the view that the entire universe worked wonderfully like clockwork in its predictability and certainty. But early in the 20th century physicists such as Niels Bohr and Heisenberg found evidence to suggest that in the field of Quantum Physics dealing with small particles there exists an underlying randomness, probability, unpredictability, and uncertainty rather than clockwork regularity.

And, of course, the physicists experimenting with cosmic rays have come to accept that they are not either particles of waves, but that they are both particles <u>and</u> waves.

✳   ✳   ✳   ✳   ✳

How Probable Is Probability

140 Some years past a journalist wrote a column speculating about the people who would jump from the Brooklyn Bridge. The statistics of past years indicated that some would, because each year some do. But there was no way of predicting what any particular persons would do so. And even those who did make the leap did not know they would be among the jumpers when the article was written. We come to see that statistics is a tool that can predict somewhat of the nature of people and the things we can expect they might do. That, based on information concerning what we know many of them have been doing.

We needs must acknowledge that behavior is not always predictable. The determining factors are many, variable, and largely unknowable as it pertains to cause and effect in the life of the individual. Though Newton Physics deals with certainties, Quantum Physics has subsequently come forth to make us aware of the uncertainties of matter and energy. And one's individual course through live makes us decidedly aware of the uncertainties we are inevitably to encounter in our day-by-day lives. Though the destiny of mankind in general be predictable on the basis of statistics, yet, we are wont individually to believe that one's personal destiny is to some extent in his own hands. We are generally enough content with personal flexibility in the living of our lives. And have had to endure enough of misadventures in bureaucratic government that we aspire for as little of is as is possibly. The notion of an ideal utopia of a planned and placid society of mindless robots is quite unrealistic.

We may come eventually to realize that the makeup of our own nature may prove to be such that our processes of thought do not correspond to the processes of nature sufficiently to permit of our thinking about it at all well. Stopped therefore from pushing our philosophical inquiries very far by limitation of our biological design and construction. Doomed perhaps to live forever with irresolvable paradoxes.

"It is not necessary to solve with absolute finality the metaphysical problem of the freedom to the will any more that it is necessary to solve the paradoxes of time and space in order to live in both." Belief in some sort of autonomy is not incompatible with what is actually known about the behavior of either animate or inanimate matter.

❋   ❋   ❋   ❋   ❋

Realism

Consider next what we name as **realism**. What is real as opposed to what is illusion. (Let us cast aside that which is delusional-mere erroneous belief as opposed now to the misperception of appearance.) We confront the entire world including our own individual physical being and come immediately to accept the information of our sensory system which suggests what we might now name as **naïve realism**. The notion that reality is just what our senses portray to our untutored perceptions. Gradually however our experimentation and experience of life begins to suggest other possibilities. Towards that end we needs must always to be in the process of probing with our additional senses and focused attention to verify and elucidate a more precise nature to all that we encounter. Testing it with the powers of our several senses. And weighing with our powers of the rational mind. Reason, analysis, and logic. What appears harmless is sometimes actually harmful-and even often immediately so. We are confronted with skilled magicians who stump us with illusions. We discover that many a person and not infrequently even sometimes a friend or a family member is apt to deceive us. And we must finally acknowledge and delve into the possibility of <u>analytical realism</u>. That material things and conceptual matters are commonly something other than what their appearance would suggest to us on first-impressions. A double entendre between the appearance and the reality behind that appearance. The loose fit between the 'mind' and the world. We gradually learn to recognize clues which suggest that in this instance or that, we must be ready to doubt naïve realism and resort to an analytic mode in order to come to some more pragmatically workable or reasonable conclusion. Our health and well-being is fragile and often endangered in this difficult and unforgiving world as we learn to be ever more alert to the covert as well as the overt causes of the dangers and problems which confront us in our passage through life.

From birth, one's (intangible) conscious awareness gradually comes to identify with one's (tangible) physical being in the world and universe of physicality. The intangible mind becomes the final arbiter concerning the realities of the physical world-as well as of matters intangible. We come to perceive that the foundations of that tangible world are rooted in the reality of cause and effect, but yet must come eventually to perceive another more subtle reality: that coincidence in time and place is by no means an always irrefutable proof of cause and effect relationship. Often we are unable to locate and identify the cause of a particular effect. When remote in time or space, one is apt to suppose of mystical unseen causes. But many unseen causes are hidden only because of the limitations of our senses despite the reality of their existence (i.e. electromagnetism and gravity). Realities which we first come to acknowledge by inference. And there is that which is both unseen and unreal which is mistakenly inferred to be real cause, such as superstition, magic, and perhaps the gods of supernaturalism.

Whether or not there be either a something-or a nothing; there exists in the abstract, the eternal why?. Science does not much concern itself with the philosophical why, but more instead with the what, the how, the quantity, and to what effect. Also abiding even were there an absence of the-something, there would yet exist abstractions of that which is immaterial, such as numbers, vague possibilities, value, quality, beauty, etc. Abstractions with and to which the immaterial function of mind has some access and dealings. In the presence of a material something, the WHY would seem necessarily to fractionate into a subset of questions: what? how? when?, where?, and who? And once we concede the reality of the material something, we must concede the necessity of what we call time, and space. For our experience of 'the-something' directly informs us of the inevitability of the change of material substance that needs must progress through the reality of the medium of time and of space, regardless of its cause. A cause which is always inevitable.

* * * * *

Concept Of Immortality

Recall that it was Socrates who seems to have originated the conception of 'the immortal soul'. That conception seems to have dominated European thinking ever since. For more than 2000 years it has been the standing assumption of civilized European man that each has a soul. It remains an assumption. Nothing more. An intangible something which is alleged to be the seat of his normal waking intelligence and moral character; "and that, since this 'soul' is either identical with himself or at any rate the most important thing about him, his supreme business in life is to make the most of it and to the do the best for it." (see Taylor)

"The direct influence, indeed, which has done most to make the doctrine [of the soul] so familiar to ourselves is that of Christianity." For when Christianity arrived into the Greco-Roman world it found that the general conception of the soul-which it needed-had already been prepared for it by philosophy-by Socrates. "It is absent from the literature of earlier times." "Socrates created the intellectual and moral tradition by which European man has ever since lived." (p. 79 Taylor)

* * * * *

I was recently taken aback to hear from an old acquaintance specifically telling me that he considered himself to be immortal. I ought not to have been surprised that he would state it so bluntly. For the matrix of most religions seem actually to imply that human immortality is the case. That, even though I have spent my entire life with the notion that perhaps the whole human race has always acknowledged that we are all mere mortals. Or, is it more prevalently believed by the religious, that like the Titans, man is first conceived by the gods and thereby has acquired something akin to the nature of demigods? A sort of reward for good deeds, good behavior, or for being steadfast in even unproven belief.

✳   ✳   ✳   ✳   ✳

Mortal Immortality?

Johnathan Swift's, *Gulliver's Travels* tells an interesting story that gives us some cause to ponder the question of a mortal immortality. Gulliver iterates the tale from one of the imaginary lands which he has visited. A tale of the rare but occasional individual who once having been born, is destined to a mortal immortality here on earth. These, he called Struldbruggs. They, were said to be born exempt from that universal calamity of human nature-death. Gulliver supposes that they would have minds free and disengaged, without the weight and depression of spirits caused by the continual apprehension of death. Gulliver speculates as to the great advantages of these people to themselves and to the nation in general, supposing they would be wise and able counselors as a counterbalance to the young men of court who are too opinionated and volatile to be guided by the sober dictates of their seniors. Gulliver postulates that were he so fortunate as one of these Struldbruggs, that he would first resolve by all arts and methods to procure wealth and riches to himself. So that he might in the space of perhaps 200 years become the wealthiest man in the kingdom. [Such as George Soros, Bill Gates or Warren Buffet] And that from earliest youth he would apply himself to the study of arts and sciences so as to excel above all others in learning and become a living treasure of knowledge and wisdom. Supposing that the youth of the kingdom might then cluster about him [as to Socrates] to become well instructed and informed citizens of what would then become a very enlightened political state to which ever more knowledge and technological advance would accumulate. That wealth, wisdom, peace, and enlightened government might then radiate outward to encompass the entire earth to the benefit of all mankind.

Gulliver was informed however of his naivety. Was informed that in reality, the fate of these immortals was rather much of a burden and disadvantage to themselves. That these Struldbruggs had not only the follies and infirmities of other old men, but many more which arose from the dreadful prospect of never dying. They were peevish, covetous, morose, vain, and incapable of friendship; and dead to all natural affection. Envy and impotent desires were their prevailing passions. That those objects against which their envy seems principally directed were the vices of the younger sort, and the deaths of the old. That they became cut off from all possibility of pleasure. They lamented that others might pass on to that 'harbor-of-rest', to which they might themselves never hope. Thought of themselves as condemned-without any fault of their own-to perpetual continuance in the world. They are become deprived of their age mates and become forgetful of the words of their own language. Thus, they have no-one with whom to converse. They can never amuse themselves with reading, because their memory will not serve to carry them from the beginning of a sentence to the end.

Being informed of this reality, Gulliver then became of the opinion that no tyrant could invent a fate so evil into which he would not run with pleasure-from such a life as physical mortal-immortality.

That at least is what Swift has to say on the matter, and since it is his story, he can fictionalize its 'actualities' how-so-e'er he pleases. But we as readers of his fiction can as easily suppose that matters might turn out differently. Suppose for example that the immortal Struldbruggs as such were given 'eternal youth' and concomitant good health. Then matters might be more in keeping with his initial speculations.

✳   ✳   ✳   ✳   ✳

Academicians or Old Age?

From Swift's *Gulliver's Travels*
[condition reminiscent of old age?]

As Gulliver was disembarking into the midst of a crowd, he noted some with peculiarities. They were as astonished of his appearance as was he of theirs. He tells us that their heads were all reclining to either the left or the right [as though forever pondering something]. And that one of their eyes were turned inward [suggesting a state of continuous deep introspection] while the other eye turned upward [as though to suggest a perpetual state of postulating something or another].

He noted that some appeared to be servants who each carried a sort of balloon on a stick. And that each balloon contained a few peas or pebbles. With these gentle rattlers the servant at times flapped the mouth, an ear, or about the eye of a person they were attending. Gulliver was told that the minds of these foremost citizens being so attended were so much absorbed with internal speculations that they neither spoke nor attended to what others were saying to them unless they were to be gently tapped on the mouth, an ear, or near the eye by the servant attending them. A signal or reminder that they were to speak or listen to what was being said-or to take visual notice or something or another. The were so self absorbed that they could not walk the streets or make visits without the aid of their attendant thus to alert them. They being so deep in thought that there was always eminent danger of their taking a nasty tumble or unwittingly bumping other pedestrians off the curb and into the street unless their attention be so aroused by the servant attendant.

✳   ✳   ✳   ✳   ✳

Intelligent Universe

Information and Intelligence are part of the world and universe, not alien to it. It is nature becoming aware of itself. Insofar as we on planet earth can tell, Homo sap. is its most advanced nearly complete embodiment of intelligence. "Science and philosophy are different kinds of intelligent enquiry, yet both are concerned with the attempt at explaining the world." (Abel)

There is but a loose fit between the mind and the world. Philosophical questions and riddles sometimes have no solution at all, which is part of what one means by 'a loose fit between mind and the world. (p. xxiv Abel)

"The word Philosophy literally means 'the love of wisdom'. The aim of Philosophy is to account for all that there is, <u>and only what there is</u>." (p. 3 Able) Aims pursued with critical analysis and speculative insight. (p. xix Able*)*

<u>Belief</u> is thinking with assent. (p. 79 Abel) Belief is a disposition and attitude or act of the mind. It is not a kind of knowledge, but merely a requirement or oath by which people assume license to claim as absolute knowledge, that which is otherwise unverifiable. Thus, belief is a necessary condition for knowledge, but not a sufficient one. (p. 23 Abel)

<u>Faith</u> is voluntary, since it is not compelled by facts, says Aquinas. Pragmatic, in that it is at least a comforting delusion, one might say.

<u>Logic</u> is the concerted effort to verify with valid evidence or arguments. In any given instance, it may or may not succeed. (p. 56 Abel)

Besides the abstract ever present question of **why**, there are other abstract conceptions that exist independently of whether there be either a-something or a-nothing. Such would be the conception of numbers and their relatedness to one another. In the presence of a-something, these abstract numbers have a tendency to transform (through man's variable powers of reason, logic, experience, and experiments in reality) into a 'mathematics' of which we mere mortals (ourselves the product of a lengthy evolutionary process) have eventually become aware, and find ourselves using math as a tool to our ever advancing science and civilization, and in our study and evaluation of the nature of reality.

We are advised to be cautious with the word '<u>reality</u>' as it tends to become a term of praise rather than a useful descriptive concept. It "carries an agreeable afflatus without dependence on any definite meaning" says Morris Cohen (p. 3 Able)

why? what? how? when?, where?, and who? All such intangible questions abide within 'the mind of mankind in toto' of we mere mortals. A mortal being can develop but a pittance of one's potential talent. And each can come to possess but little of the skills, information, and knowledge which has been so slowly and laboriously acquired through thousands of generations to what has become a large grand sum-total which the minds of men currently possess and are partly transcribed into tomes and libraries of writings. Homo sapiens seemingly the only species to have acquired the skills of language, and writings, within a cultural tradition that passes the knowledge and the lessons of yester-years onto each subsequent generations. Thereby endowing each subsequent generation of the species with access to knowledge and information (as well as honest fiction, misinformation and delusional knowledge) that enables the race to delve, ponder, and sort through ever more deeply into the vast unknown in quest of a progressing enlightenment. A sorting and culling that requires the exercise of the powers of reason and a first-hand experience of the nature of the reality in which we are immersed.

> The mind was built for mighty freight
> For dread occasion planned
> Yet often floundering at sea
> Ostensibly on land!
> Emily Dickinson

"In the transmission of human culture there is always the attempt to pass on to the next generation the skills and values of the parents." But that goal always inevitably falls short of its full intention "because cultural transmission is geared to learning-not to congenitally inherited DNA." (p. 52 Bateson)

Mere Mortals

Tangible And Intangible

The abstractions (numbers, value, quality, beauty, possibility, process, time, space, existence, being, mind, etc.) are from the realm of intangible. But through the medium of brain and mind, they apply equally to both the-something (tangible) and the-nothingness (intangible), so that the primordial nothingness must eventually be recognized in its co-existence with the something. <u>The real world of our first-hand experience is a something where the objects, ideas, processes, values, beings, and other abstractions can play out into material existence and action</u>. And where numbers become the mathematics that theoretically underlies the structure of the material something.

Planetary gravity, heat, and pressure transform and sort the spectrum of molecules into minerals, ores, liquids, and gases. The rare planet such as earth is of fortuitous size and situated fortuitously in orbit about a secondary star as a source of heat and energy. And earth ends up 'as though' it were 'fine tuned' to permit not only for the evolution of rudimentary life, but permissive even of the slow evolution from rudimentary life to progressively advanced life forms. "As though to be 'fine turned'" is a concept posited by religious creationists to support their religious beliefs. But scientifically it is more correct to say "fortuitously permissive to evolution of life" in that it permits of being free of religious prejudice.

The abstract of 'possibility' has had to precede the tangibility of plasma particles in 'the big bang'. Particles which have progressed to molecules in the process of cooling. They in turn have progressed to stars; to secondary molecules; to secondary stars; and to planets. And from the inorganic of molecules fortuitously situated upon a star-and-planet relationship, has arisen the organic primitive <u>life based upon the peculiar properties of the carbon atom</u>, in the presence of available space, time, light, water, and oxygen. Carbon molecules, have a unique ability to combine into a very plethora of different carbon-based molecules. Among them are the molecules which are the material basis of all primitive and advanced life forms on earth.

"Since all organisms have descended from a common ancestor, it may be said that the biosphere as a whole began to philosophize when humanity was born. If the rest of 'creation' can be thought of as the body (of the universe), we (Homo sapiens) might then be thought of as its 'mind'." "Thus, it is our place in nature, viewed from an ethical perspective, to think about the creation and to protect the living planet." (p. 132 Wilson) A matter that would have been of no concern when human populations were too small to impact a relatively vast environment and equilibrium of life forms.

※　※　※　※　※

Tangible Link To Intangible

One might question as to whether perhaps the-nothing and the-something coexist. The great divide between the tangible and the intangible. I am inclined to suppose that they do. <u>The function of the brain appears to be the connecting link between the two. And our internal lives are regularly involved in both spheres. Our lives straddle that great divide.</u> And we are constantly in dilemma account of it.

And physicists claim to have evidence that particles do spontaneously appear-out of the-nothingness into the-something (and back again). How could that be?, unless the-nothing were already in co-existence with the-something. And how curiously similar to my own to my own being which-unasked for-has suddenly appeared and set out upon my brief journey through life. And will ere long suddenly again disappear into the void.

Our mortal flesh is in, and is an intricate part of the tangible world and universe in which we are imbedded. But there is a second and intangible component to our human being and the universe. That component is the metaphysical conceptual realm of idea. Brain is the organ of man's physical and physiological being which generates the mind and consciousness. A mind and consciousness that enables us to function simultaneously in both the realm of the tangible and the intangible

The four elementary particles are said to be the neutron, the proton, the electron, and the photon. Of those, only the photon is said to be immaterial. (see *Music of the Spheres*, by Guy Murchie) That again would imply the interaction between the-nothing and the-something.

✳   ✳   ✳   ✳   ✳

Challenge Of Infancy

Though the newborn infant undoubtedly has visual perception it might be said that technically the infant does not begin to see until perhaps several weeks of age. For it has no background of experience upon which to interpret its visual or auditory sensations. But in its helpless dependency the newborn is instinctively avid soon to recognize and begin to read the language of the eyes and face of its mother. The reciprocity of eye contact soon becomes manifest. The elementary language of the eyes persists throughout life. "Drink to me only with thine eyes, and I will pledge with mine..." [Song To Celia by Ben Jonson]. Facial expressions take on an expanded meaning to the infant, and verifies the language of the eyes. Posture and poses contribute more, and eventually we come to the phenomenon of the mime. [i.e. a Charley Chaplin] The child touches, tastes, and smells whatever comes into his reach to verify unto himself the nature of all things. This additional information alters and improves the accuracy and quality of his visual and auditory perceptions of the nature of the reality in his conception of the world about him.

Without any specific instruction, the neurologically intact and perceptive child rapidly acquires an elementary grasp of the spoken word and begins to verbalize by about two years of age. Gathering meaning from what is seen and heard, the child soon has the beginnings of a small vocabulary and begins to grasp the rudiments of the structure of language. And not long after, begins then to evolve to himself the rudiments of <u>a theory of</u> intangible <u>mind</u>. Becomes conscious of mind long before he becomes conceptually aware of it. Begins to perceive meaning from interactional situations to which he is audience and participant.

Language exponentially facilitates the learning process and the accumulation of information and knowledge. With enlarging vocabulary the evolving mind of the child can soon question and express doubt. Becomes a student. Possible then to probe the wisdom of the minds of those of one's milieu. Possible then to communicate the intangible concept, idea, and theory.

※　※　※　※　※

Security And Reproduction

There exists also a fundamental human craving for security. And beyond that, is deeply imbedded the instinct of procreation which appears to have intermittent precedence even over our native sense of curiosity. The nature of reality seems as though to have little concern for the life, agonies, and death of the individual. As though its one goal in the game of life were that of reproduction-to permit of an ongoing dialectical experimentation in the evolution of our thought, and of our species. Perhaps not much concern even for species, when we take into account that 99% of all species ever to have existed, have gone extinct.

The fundamental long term urge and seeming mission of each new mortal is at last the mandate of procreation. Though by no means is each destined to accomplish that.

Among our human species, our new-born lives are like unto a finished new fabric of tightly woven filaments of brightly stained color. From this fabric our lives are shaped and patched together as we molt into the mature adult status of our life-cycle. One might liken the fibers of cloth onto the bone, tendon, and cells of our human anatomy. And might liken the colors of our analogy onto the mental aspects of one's being-mind, consciousness, thought, emotion….

And we live out our brief lives in a sea of space-time, subject to the physical elements of this world and universe. The fabric of one's being becomes threadbare and the colors fade. We strain, wear, and degrade the physical elements of our existence as we struggle against those forces of nature to grow, patch, and mend our frames. Struggle to maintain our brief lives from day to day. Eking out a subsistence from an Earth that yields only reluctantly the animalcular prey, and the fruits and grains from which we may stoke the fires of our metabolism, thought, motion, and action within ourselves continuously to gather and harvest onto the self-serving necessity of our personal ongoing existence.

And we find it necessary to compete (as a species of wild, powerful, and wily creatures) with other species for the meat, as well as for the grain and fruit to maintain ourselves. This, while also competing with individuals and other tribes of our own species for the always limited supply of necessities of space, physiologic needs, wants, and desires.

Always faced with necessity, wish, and dilemma. Not only must we hunt and gather, but are always first at pains to discern a plan and a method for how to go about the business of acquiring that which we need and desire. Must then exert and risk our physical being to tediously acquire our necessary skills and a pragmatically useful accumulation of information towards that end. Must collate our thought and concepts with studied perceptions and determination, to concentrate the essential elements of the unformed jumble of each enigma and dilemma to conceive of what must be done. To imagine how that may be accomplished, and what device and tools we must shape to achieve our lately conceived objective.

Must wrest from nature the process and use of fire. And the valued necessities of shelter and clothing, against the elements of nature. Must devise and utilize tools for hunting and for our defense against the predatory creatures of the vast mysterious and forbidding jungles of this world.

Our instinct and determination to survive is with us so long as we can garner the necessities of life and endure life's agonies. Inescapable is our need for every consecutive breath and the urgent intermittent demand of our innards for the morsel of sustenance.

✳   ✳   ✳   ✳   ✳

Infant to Mother

Each newborn human being is but 'a quivering lump of clay not far removed from a beast that day' with no hope nor possibility of surviving beyond perhaps but a day or two if left to its own devices and mere latent possibilities. A bundle of autonomic functions, needs, wants, and demands-but having (in infancy) no power within itself to supply even its necessities. A CNS with merely latent potential for thought. Dare we call this primitive jungle of dim perceptions anything more than a prelude to the evolution of a mind? The potentially intangible mind, devoid of any physical content either in its beginnings, its middle, or its end. The intangible nature of the mere potential of mind. Mind potential, wed to the tangible lump of clay with also naught more than the potential of possibility. How then shall this lowly combination of potential survive, and how then ever so slowly shaped for the possibility of a fruition into a maturity of being?

One is precipitated into a world and universe which permits, constrains and limits one's own being, yet upon which he is dependent and with which one must come to terms. Can it be said that the world and universe has both an intangible mind and a physicality of its own with continuous change (manifest as the forever inscrutable 'dialectical materialism') which one needs must immediately and constantly explore; and with which one must compromise. The infant would seem to have been born with an aggressive instinct to develop his own potential and an avid willingness to explore and make conquest by discovering the physical reality, rules, and laws of nature.

The newborn infant of our species, born into our world has an undeveloped brain, but does not yet have even the potential to survive on his own without the care of the group or family into which he is precipitated-and dependant primarily upon the mother. Neither does the infant have more than just the potential for a conceptual mind (**a function** of CNS), though he does possess the anatomical brain and the potential for 'mind' (through time, experience, and reciprocity with other minds). And has potential to evolve unto himself an ever widening consciousness and a variable ability to focus his waking conscious mind. In the presence of a nurturing family and the culture thereof, the infant promptly sets about the task of learning the language which connects him to those who answer his 'prayer' requests and provide his comfort and sustenance.

The infant begins evolving onto himself a mind; and a consciousness of himself-and of the world about him. An ongoing process that continues forward long into his adult years as a consequence of his day-by-day interactions with the world, with society, and with the minds and persons of his milieu.

Consider then the eternal life-giving mother. With what purpose has nature endowed her? No natural purpose perhaps, other than to initiate and produce yet generation after generation endlessly into yet another existence, and into an unforgiving world and universe. Herself, born and shaped by a mother before. Cast by fate into this endless cycle. Constrained by the wonders of dying and birth to but a brief span. "Inheritor of a few years and sorrows".

Having then produced the quivering lump of clay, the mother's genetic instinct is to nurture this each newborn life. In like manner as the cold and hungry adult must cherish the ever scanty sparks and nurture the ever dying embers into a useful flame. A bond of one generation to the next. Even without the mother's awareness of that instinct that yet abides within her. A mother's purpose is both in the generation and sustaining of new life. The child requires the mother, just as the mother requires the child to maintain some vague sense of purpose.

Besides producing the new life, her task is then to sustain and to shape that newborn life. A first phase of nine months, and the long-term 15 year investment in the shaping and nurturing the lump of clay into a self-sustaining being and a possible link to yet another subsequent generation.

"Thought is life and strength and breath. And the want of thought is death." (Blake) When I was a child I thought of myself as a physical being, and never gave thought to the mental aspect of my being. As says Descartes, "I think therefore I am". Slowly through the passing years I too have come grudgingly to think of myself much more essentially as an intangible mind. Like Siddhartha, ever and all about me I see and acknowledge the agonizing of hunger, sickness, pain, old age, and death. And I come late and reluctantly to see the signs of that reality accumulating within myself. Just as in the case of our hypothetical mother, I also come to recognize that perhaps my natural physical being has had no other natural purpose beyond that of procreation. I perceive that my aging frame is beginning already to fossilize. And that even surely I too needs must leave my out-grown shell upon the shores of life's un-resting sea.

And yet, as a primitive people and tribe make slow progress towards a more orderly and civilized life situation, their limited life spans enlarge and the minds of men begin to delve into the intangible and conceptual of possibility, purpose, ideals, value, creativeness, quality etc. Individuals become gradually able to begin to aspire to other goals and purpose in life than simply that of procreation and the daily struggle for life. Hopefully then to acquire some time and freedom to quest for goals and purpose of their own making.

✳   ✳   ✳   ✳   ✳

"Being"

Existence Versus "Being"

Inanimate molecules evolve first gradually into primitive life with "existence" but not yet endowed with any sense of conscious 'being'. That which is inorganic, and the rudimentary forms of animalcular organic life possess only an 'existence'. In the matter of <u>mere existence</u> we have reference to such living forms as plants and the lesser animalcule such as one-celled microbes, flat-worms, earthworms, insects, etc. They live, grow, and reproduce, but we do not conceive that they ruminate about a past nor contemplate a future. The life that they live is <u>always only in the ever present moment</u>-a "crack of light between two eternities of darkness". That is to say that they have 'existence'. We conceive of their acts and movement as being grounded and genetically inherited as instincts and reflex behaviors.

Primitive life progresses then to advanced life. And we are inclined to suppose that only the more advanced forms of life have conscious awareness of 'mind' possessed of thought and conscious '**being**'. We of species <u>Homo sapiens</u> and probably other higher forms of life <u>have both existence AND 'being'</u> in that we do ruminate upon our existence in the bygone past of our yesterdays; and regularly contemplate a near and a distant future of tomorrow and beyond. That is to say we of the human species have 'being' as well as existence. A "being" derived from a neurologically evolved central-nervous-system which we call a brain or a CNS. And the individual of our species has gradually begun to conceive or regard one's self as being in part, as much an 'intangible mind'; as well as a 'being' also of tangible flesh-and-blood existence. 'Beings', in and as a part of a physical world and universe of the ever present here-and-now. We human beings do contemplate and concern ourselves with the realties of the ever present here and now-as well as with the intangibility of things that are only conceptual (i.e. a past and future that do not exist in the present moment).

The concept of "consciousness was imported to play in the mental world the part analogously played by light in the mechanical [tangible] world" in which we exist. [p. 159 Ryle] But the fact and function of consciousness was present and active in mankind long before it has come to be conceptually recognized or named as such.

✳   ✳   ✳   ✳   ✳

Mind

"If a sequence of events combines a random component with a selective process so that only certain outcomes of the random are allowed to endure, that sequence is said to be <u>stochastic</u>." (p. 253 Bateman) One-celled life comes into 'existence' from the earth's natural physical and chemical components. That life has only come eventually through evolution to be manifest as the structure and function of simple 'existence'. One-celled life forms having once come into 'existence', then by virtue of a stochastic dialectic law of nature, nature's idea gives rise to the multi-cellular. And from the multi-cellular comes next the segmentation and differentiation into tissues of specialized function.

Ultimately a specialized nervous system evolves and begins to coordinate the functions of a simple life form into a coordinated existence on the simple 'stimulus-and-response' principle. And from that nervous system there begins to arise some progressive physical and functional enlargement that eventually becomes the reptilian Central Nervous System with naked reflex, instinct, and emotion combined with special senses such as vision, hearing, sense of touch etc. A combination of function with the rudiments of what might be called a dim consciousness of individual being. Atop of that reptilian CNS much later gradually evolves the ever enlarging Cerebral Cortex of mankind, the function of which is eventually able to conceive of the intangible concept from the philosopher's realm of 'idea'. Concepts such as intangible id, ego, and superego, which we begin to conceive of as an allegorical system of counterbalanced qualities of man's intangible 'mind'. A CNS, which advances ever further in sophistication and is enabled to speculate upon the abstract. It's enlarging functional capabilities we begin to conceive as being imbued with mind and consciousness; and later, a conscious awareness of its own inner self. Begins to weave conceptual elements of the abstract into its imaginative speculations and motivations. Possessing then that intangible entity we begin to name as a 'conscious mind'. A mind is not a substance or a place, but rather a function of a differentiate and perceptive brain. An abstracted mind and consciousness which when once eventually generated by the brain, begins in turn to assume some reciprocity of control and ordering of the brain's potential for disciplined calculation such that the 'flesh-and-blood' body and brain begin to do the bidding of its sublimated intangible mind to some variable extent. A brain thus somewhat conceptually once removed-from a chaos of mere reflexes, raw instincts, and its stream of sensory perceptions. A sense of order comes eventually to function conceptually as a conscious mind-which we many come to regard as 'the essence' of a person's being.

Unbenounced to the individual, one's mind begins to abstract itself some little conceptual distance from its source. That source being a tangible brain, body, and one's personal experience of and in the world. Mind, generated and thus inseparably entwined with that source. Mind to influence and be influenced by that source. A mind aware-that it must live, prosper, and die with the physical aspect of that body which is its only source of subsistence, and its only ultimate source of experience and knowledge of the world and universe. Mind must come to a mutually beneficial truce with its intermediary physical body; even perhaps accept some compromise with "the Heavy Bear" aspect of a body's person. Potentially always judgmental, mind must endure with some patience the body's sometimes counterproductive reflexes, instinct, emotion, and autonomic excesses.

The mind with some luck inherits a body that is genetically sound and derived of a caring and helpful family which is at least permissive if not encouraging of some intellectual cultural tradition; nor overly superstitious. And hopefully born into peaceful and prosperous times in a nation which is conducive to individual freedom.

The intermediary body channels into the slowly maturing mind-the influence, experience, information, training, and values to which it has been subjected. By the time the mind reaches maturity it has attained some variable capacity for reason and judgment enough to wield its influence and dominate to some greater or lesser degree over bodily habit, predisposition, reflexes, instinct, and emotion. Enough reason and judgment to temper and moderate a human being towards prudence and pragmatic course of action amid the uncertainties and dilemmas of life in a vast and complex world of challenges.

In childhood and youth a mind may be not much aware of even its own existence and potential. A mind has had to depend upon the luck of the draw as to its own body in the matter of a body's attraction to the intellectual aspects of its being. And like the body itself, the mind grows and matures only gradually. As with love, the spark of intellect may grow into a motivating disposition.

Habits, reflexes, instincts, and mind are all components that weigh into what we name as <u>character</u> and predisposition which much influence the behavior, actions, and the course of one's life.

❋　❋　❋　❋　❋

Mind at Work

The intangible rational, mature, and active mind comes to regard itself as being somewhat distinct and aloof from the tangible body. Comes to see the body, its parts, and the world objectively as well as subjectively. Comes to understand ever more clearly the meaning and certainty of bodily death. But the mind also becomes aware that it is by no means all-knowing; and that it harbors many doubts and uncertainties. The conscious mind is long aware and accustomed to its imaginative ideas and scenarios, none of which is mind ever able to explore beyond imagination, except through the intermediary body and into the tangible world. The body and the world are the mind's workshop. Most of one's imaginings have proven to be unsound, as is also a considerable portion of the 'information' and 'knowledge' to which the mind has been given access. Access only through the intermediating body and from the tangible outside world of which the body is a part. That of course includes what the eyes have read and what the ears have heard.

The mind fabricates (both consciously and unconsciously) a great many things that are not so and that do not exist. That ability and tendency comes even to be not only useful to one in the exercise of one's powers of reason-but vital. We postulate on the possible meaning of this or that fact; or the source of some noise in the dark of night, so that we can speculate on the probability of the reality-of one possibility versus another. Mind forever questioning and ever fearful of the potential for error and danger; and in quest of the validity of suppositions as we hope and attempt to comprehend the nature of an ever elusive reality.

Fact is relative to hypothesis. One's night of sleep is occasionally interrupted by 'things that go 'bump in the night'. In a state of semi-wakefulness one must ponder a bit to guess as to its cause. Worrisome? Or not? Possibilities cross one's mind. Some plausible insignificant cause will often occur to one-saving him the necessity of having to get up to investigate.

Having oft and early been surprised and come to grief from one's own naivety, we individually tend to become ever more analytical in our perceptions. Uncertainty, doubt, and skepticisms inevitably creep into one's habits and thought processes.

An Image of Truth
I place all my trust in things that I doubt,
The obvious-alone-is unclear
Certainty never know what its about,
And truth from pure chance will appear.

I'm still just a loser, although I win all.
"Good night", I say at day's dawning.
Even in bed I'm scared that I'll fall,
And I've only got plenty of nothing.
Francois Villon (1431-1483)

Science being born from curiosity, doubt, and uncertainty thus has its beginnings and its causes. Empirical experience often leads us forward into ever better, but sometimes counterproductive habits even before science may eventually present us with an informed rational to support our useful habit. Or abandon that which is unhelpful.

The mind has had continuously to sort through its uncertainty, hopes, and wishful thinking. Yet remains ever capable of clinging to comforting unverifiable belief when certainly eludes one.

It is clear of course that the mind, ideas, and conceptions belong to the category of intangible entities. And that they originate to man's awareness and persist as products of living tissues of the neurons and brains of mankind in general. We might name the process as '<u>thought</u>', by which these intangibles become known to ourselves in consequence of the metabolic processes of neurons. That is to say, that one of the functions of the neurons of the brain is the production and organization of these intangibles into the general concept of what we call intangible '**mind**'. Within this intangible package we call "mind", are other conceptual qualities such as consciousness, sub-consciousness, memory, imagination, ideas, ideals, value, numbers, quality, beauty, possibility, etc. So it can be said that <u>the tangible living tissues of the brain</u> generates <u>the conception of intangible "mind" with the quality of consciousness</u>. And it is within this intangible mind that we <u>imaginatively manipulate</u>

intangible symbols and scenarios to produce modified and expanded concepts and ideas which motivate and inspire other neuronal processes within the brain to intermittently precipitate some action of the tangible body into and within the real world-of which the tangible body is a part. We have thus a reciprocity between the tangible and the intangible which is dependent upon the ongoing metabolic activity of the neurons and the brain. We know this imaginative manipulation of the conceptually intangible to occur because we all regularly involve ourselves with this process that we call thought or thinking. Even just to say something aloud or in one's head is an evidence of thought.

Clearly these conceptual intangibles such as ideas, ideals, knowledge, and beliefs contribute to the formation of one's character and often motivate and inspire you and I (and mankind in general) in the course of our lives. Clearly these intangibles guide us in our general behavior, into an occasional course of action, and into the invention of the material goods with which we surround ourselves. And in the use of which we forever strive and often succeed in easing many of the natural difficulties we encounter in our lives.

In my own experience (and based on what I can see, hear, and read from the experience of others) the thoughts, ideas, and concepts with which we deal are at inception most generally fragmented and lacking in organization so that a great much of it is fleeting in nature and comes to serve no useful purpose to us. Yet, some of that which is fragmented like a jigsaw puzzle and unorganized and which commonly ends up being useless can be made conceptually informative, interesting, and useful to us. If perchance we are motivated to trouble ourselves and take the time and invest our effort into an imaginative manipulation of these fragments-into a conceptual order and form that can prove fruitful. This, by the exercise of one's capacity for thought.

Such "thought experiments" as we hear about (i.e. those in the life of Einstein pertaining to 'relativity') make us conceptually conscious that we too regularly conduct these same sorts of process, to which we may never previously have put a name. Thought Experiments.

The Brain—is wider than the Sky
For—put them side by side
The one the other will contain
With ease—and You—besides

The Brain is deeper than the sea
For—hold them—Blue to Blue
The one the other will absorb
As Sponges—Buckets—do.
. . . .
Emile Dickinson

It remains yet not comprehended as to how tangible neurological tissue comes to possess a reciprocity of communication with the realm of the intangible. A process that seems probably to be largely facilitated by memory and imagination. Here the die-hard Cartesians may be wont once more to slip in their 'immortal inner man'. But there is no evidence of any such 'inner man' and nothing is to be gained by clumsily forcing a fictional factor into the equation. It only places the unexplained matter one step more distantly removed from an explanation. And it presents one with yet another difficulty which persons will be reluctant to own.

For the reality is that mankind is not alone in the possession of a tangible brain. A brain that also deals with matters from the realm of the intangible. All of mankind are regular witness to the fact that in this matter, all mammals and creatures far on down the phylogenetic tree regularly demonstrate this conceptual ability in their behaviors-even though lacking the human advantage in the matter of language. "If people had had trouble thinking without language, where would their language have come from?" (p. 149 Pinker)

Yes, an ability to think that is easily seen in birds, reptiles, and noted even in the octopus and cuttlefish. If the explanation were that of an intangible 'soul' in Homos sapiens, the same reasoning would suggest that these other creatures too each possess a 'soul'. What then has previously been proposed as being unique in mankind, would appear rather to be a quality that differs (although considerably in degree) from the beasts of the field, the oceans, and the jungles of this world.

✳ ✳ ✳ ✳ ✳

Inner Voice

As to Language it seems to me that in my thought processes, I am continuously silently speaking to myself internally. Perhaps that is an erroneous conclusion reinforced to me by the fact that I have done considerable writing in my lifetime. And I am certain that as I write, I definitely am vocalizing internally the words just before and as they appear on the screen before me. In fact, as I ponder the matter it seems to me that I am silently shaping my words and sentences with my tongue and voice box.

And often out of the realm of the subconscious, "through the deep caves of thought I hear a voice that rings..." (*The Chambered Nautilus*) A voice that annoyingly and reiteratively disturbs me with scenarios, chatter, and cajoling. Not infrequently delaying my journey into a night of sweet slumber.

Willyard tells us of Lev Vygotsky, a Russian psychologist who proposed in the 1930s that our inner voice evolves when we are still children. That we first learn to use speech to communicate with others. And soon, we begin to speak to ourselves, too. We've all heard children talk to themselves as they build Lego toys or cook imaginary foods. Vygotsky says that those private conversations begin to take place silently inside our heads. The theory seems to me intuitive.

"The trick of talking to oneself in silence is acquired neither quickly nor without effort; and it is a necessary condition of our acquiring that we should have previously learned to talk intelligently aloud and have heard and understood other people dong so." (p. 27 Ryle)

Willyard tells us of Psychologist, Charles Fernyhough, (Durham University in Britain) who studies the relationship between inner speech and the hearing of voices. Fernyhough suggests the obvious; that "inner speech is just private speech that has been fully internalized" That "the stuff that you do in your head is basically a version of the stuff you used to do out loud as a kid."

Because one's internal dialogue is private it is difficult to study. "There are good reasons to think that by attempting to observe this private experience, you invariably alter its content." "Try having a thought and documenting it at the same time, and you'll begin to understand the problem scientists are up against." Vygotsky himself is said to have complained that "the area of inner speech is one of the most difficult to investigate." Recently several researchers have actually begun to gather information about the voices inside our heads. "To elucidate more clearly just what the inner voice is—and what it isn't."

Willyard indicates that Psychologist Hurlburt is trying to make sense of our common inner experience by cataloging hundreds of individual experiences. His subjects are given beepers "programmed to sound an alarm several times a day as they go about their lives. When his subjects get a beep, they make a detailed record of what was going on internally at that moment." Then, at the end of each day, Hurlburt interviews these subjects in an effort to "tease apart the actual experiences of each one's inner voice"-from their presuppositions about that inner voice. Often, there aren't words. "Some thoughts take the form of pictures, sensations, or have no form at all." The inner voice is reported "in about a quarter of the reports of his patients' experiences." Its frequency varies widely from person to person. Some people seem never to talk to themselves. Others claim to chatter nearly constantly. One "reported that she was engaged in inner speech 94 percent of the time."

I've always assumed my inner voice babbles pretty much constantly, but often what I am inwardly perceiving are perhaps not words at all. Perhaps just fragments of scenarios, or vague mullings over slights, hurt feelings, wishes, and vague hopes.

So why does this inner voice choose to appear on some occasions and remain mute on others? It typically appears "when you're really worried, or really anxious." Albarracin and her colleagues suggest that negative situations and internal struggles tend to elicit a "splitting of the mind" that transforms the inner voice into something of a surrogate questioning or counseling parent. (see Willyard, Cassandra)

✳   ✳   ✳   ✳   ✳

One wonders how those who are both deaf and dumb are able to read silently to themselves without internal speech. If they are lip readers, do they then visualize lip movements as they indulge in thought? If they are also blind but have learned Brail Print, do they have tactile perceptions as they think? Perhaps if accustomed to the use of sign language, they keep their hands hidden from observation when they are silently talking to themselves or imagines them from his memory.

In short, I am left to wonder if Human beings could have any organized thought whatsoever if they had never acquired some kind of language. Without language, perhaps one could learn nothing whatsoever except by mimicry or by trial and error? Or by the correlation of memory of past experience with present situational encounter.

I gather then that I am not alone in my impression that my own thought processes are commonly mediated by language. We are informed that persons who are conversant in two languages have their internal conversations in their native dominant language. Perhaps some of my thought proceeds silently? As dreams seem to. And as brute animal certainly must. But, of course, dreams are more of the nature of watching and attending a movie than of formulating one's own thoughts, ideas, and utterances.

Children first learn to read by reading aloud. And it has been noted that "not until 'the middle ages' of world history did people learn to read without reading aloud." (p. 27 Ryle) It requires a considerable of time and practice before individuals are able to read silently. Are they even then perhaps reading by silently shaping their words and sentences with lips, tongue, and voice box? As the process of any one awakening thought matures in one's mind, it can be supposed to become attached to some of the available words and concepts of one's accumulating mental repertory.

Reading and writing require a great deal more of focused attention and teaching than does verbal communication. The prevalence in this world of <u>misinformation</u> is as abundant as valid information. It greatly complicates the learning process to all of humanity. A complication which at every turn consumes time and leads one astray. Time too-an essentially limiting constituent of every brief life-span. Ignorance and superstition are still the prevailing situation among the minds of even the most learned of men. But by the time a child is into the mid and late teens, most would probably have acquired enough valid information and mind/body coordination to enable them to be self supporting and fend for themselves. Yet, our society is becoming so much more technologically evolved and complex in even just the past 50 to 100 years, that ever more information and training is available. And it seems prudent for one to continue to acquire ever some little more.

As cognitive scientists have focused on the nature of the mind, they have come to characterize it as a function of a physical entity-the brain at work. A wakeful mind that is continuously flooded with scenarios and information of various validity. Whether these are based on reality or entirely fictive, and whether set in the past, present, or future, these running narratives are all churned out in the mind with equal facility. "The present is constructed from the avalanche of sensations that pour into the awakened brain. Working at a furious pace, the brain summons memories to screen and help make sense of the incoming chaos. Only a minute part of incoming information is selected for higher order processing. From that part, small segments are enlisted through symbolic imagery to create the white–hot core of activity we call the conscious mind." (p. 132 Wilson)

✳   ✳   ✳   ✳   ✳

Confronting 'Mind'

As to 'theory of mind'-one perceives behind the eyes and face of those of his acquaintance, the invisible function of thought and questions just as his own mental functions are also evolving silently within himself. But of course there could be no theory of mind unless one had other minds to relate to-a consequence of psycho-sociology in action.

How to account for this development of cognitive and rational powers accumulating to what we now call 'the mind' of man? The <u>mind</u> does not have an anatomy nor a physiology, but is rather <u>a term used to designate the cognitive and intellectual functions</u> of the central nervous system. The individual skills that men and women have acquired are developed from the vast potential of talent that each might own-if only one were to devote himself attentively and repetitiously to its achievement. If only a skill were once demonstrated, the will to acquire the skill might well fire the individual to a practiced achievement. Expert instruction does facilitate and shorten the learning time of we mere mortals. The languages of the world number some 4000 (living and dead). Spoken and written language can and do facilitate and shorten the learning time even further. Powers of observation and learning-skills can likewise be stimulated, sharpened, and facilitated through verbal instruction. Life however is short, and each learning task eats into the limited span of each life, so that there is a limit to what each can acquire by learning (or experience) in the limited span of one's years. From that reality evolves what we recognize as a utility for <u>specialization</u> of skills and 'know-how' ability within the family, clan, and tribe.

We require some minimum of information and knowledge for computation and analysis such as to enable each to navigate through the enigmatic physical and conceptual realities and dilemmas of life.

<u>To know or have knowledge is an attainment</u> based on one's intellectual capacity and predisposition. Knowledge attained from one's experience of life. And commonly much enhanced by a preoccupation with reading, study, and philosophical discussion. Even we of only

average intelligence not infrequently rise to the status of students, scientists, professors, and clergy.

* * * * *

To Know How, Vs. To Know That.

It might be said that to know and to be able to use or apply that knowledge implies a deeper understanding of that information than one's ability merely to recite that knowledge. <u>To know how to</u> do things is of the nature of having acquired <u>a skill</u> or an artistic ability. Able to build or repair structures and mechanical devises. Or having acquired specific artistic technique. Skills and abilities such as one acquires by practice or gains in experience as an apprentice, for example. There is much less emphasis or preoccupation on intense reading and memorization in acquiring a particular skill or a trade. Much more emphasis on hands-on practice.

The evidence of intelligence lies in the ability to demonstrate it in one's acts, speech, or writing.

As an avocation or sideline to one's major life occupation, there is or course a great deal of cross-over between the 'egg-heads' and the technicians, for there is in the latter a requirement of some didactic preparation. And the 'intellectuals' are also put-upon for some 'know-how' in their professions and avocations.

Mankind is only gradually beginning to shed superstition and myth; and to probe into the beginnings of perceptive, rational, and analytical powers of the mind. An intellect ever more capable of perceptive awareness and eventually to become... "Sole judge of truth" (though in endless error hurled). Or, falling short of objective goals, we could yet find our species cast aside and replaced by yet an even higher form of beings. Replaced, perhaps, by creatures with greater affinity and predisposition for grand achievement.

"Skills, technique, knowledge, and information are slow to accumulate to mankind, so that the details and process accumulate only gradually to a family or tribe over a period of generations. Families, tribes, and societies of mankind have communicated skills, technique, knowledge, and information along with spoken and written language from one generation to another for thousands of years. This <u>cultural transmission of learning</u> has slowly and progressively lifted mankind to an ever greater awareness of reality, information, knowledge, technology, and science over millennia. It has broadened the horizons of his understanding just as travel has broadened the horizons of his familiarity with geography." (p. 424 Brasseur)

✵　✵　✵　✵　✵

Collective Mind

There appears then to be this thing we name as "a-collective-mind" that can be said to exist first within a close-knit group such as a family unit. And comes to exist perhaps more vaguely into a nation and a civilization. Knowledge, ideas, thoughts, concepts, and culture that is shared in common among that group from which an ancestral person had once arrived into both his physical and mental existence. A collective mind that lives on conceptually through time, and remains an ongoing slowly changing cultural influence and pattern of life which is passed on to the subsequent ongoing life of descendents. An evolving culture that survives and abides into endless generations. Just as there might be said to be a "collective mind" of family, so might it be said that there is an even broader collective mind of the entire species of mankind. A broader connection to the entire tribe and human race. The mathematics of genetic inheritance can be shown to demonstrate that even in so few as 30 generations we mere mortal men all share common ancestors. That, even though no specific individual memory seems usually to take we individuals back beyond two or three consecutive generations.

It could also be said that there is a much more vast 'universal-collective-mind of mankind' which has culturally accumulated into the society of mankind by evolving customs and experimentation with design and interaction of things and substances through the eons. The evolution of customs and the creation of the tools, weapons, and processes slowly evolves into our mortal mental conceptions along with an expanding awareness of ever more of the 'laws-of-nature'. Laws which have gradually been recognized in our personal experience as fixed certainties knowable to the 'collective-mind of man in toto'. This 'Universal Mind' has only gradually come into existence along with such abstractions as (of) value and of numbers. Numbers which evolve into a mathematics which some suggest to be at the heart of the structure of that-which-is. That 'collective-mind of man' has come to reside among Homo sapiens-a creature at the pinnacle of an awareness of conscious being.

❋   ❋   ❋   ❋   ❋

Function Of Mind

At this point one might be tempted to speculate that the intangible mind might perhaps persist, even though the physical aspects of one's being are destined to succumb and return to dust. One must, however, take cognizance of the fact that what we refer to as the 'mind' would appear to be but only a function of the tangible cerebral cortex. And that those said functions cease in consequence of death of cellular elements of the cerebral cortex, once the electrical activity of the cortical cells cease with cortical death. The cessation of that electrical phenomenon can in fact be said to be the definition of the death of individual mortal man. Once electrical cortical death has occurred, there is no possible revival of cortical function, even though the sub-cortical systems may yet persist a brief while, provided that the circulatory system and oxygenation can be reestablished without undue delay. But the cortical cells demand a continuous supply of oxygen. A crucially high demand which once interrupted for more than a few minutes, those cortical cells quickly arrive at irreversible death. The demands of the sub-tentorial CNS systems for oxygen are less sensitive to temporary oxygen deprivation. And the cells of the muscular-skeletal system are far less demanding than even this sub-cortex. Thus it is that we are occasionally confronted with a brain-dead human corpse that has residual physical 'existence' but no longer owns a 'being'.

[The tentorial membrane supports and separates the cerebral cortex above the cerebellum and brain stem. Supra-tentorial thus refers to the cerebral cortex. Which is the site of the genesis of the higher perceptive, cognitive, and intellectual functions of the brain. And from which come forth these functions and qualities that we call 'mind' and 'consciousness']

To reiterate, the human 'mind' is but a function of the supra-tentorial cerebral cortex. And that once the cortex is oxygen deprived for more than a few brief minutes, it's functional units arrive at irreversible cellular death. Its function (be it called mind or vital spirit) no longer then persists. In that very real sense, the individual intangible mind then too does cease to exist. The intangible... dependent upon the tangible? And as for the tangible... it would seem to have no potential ultimate source other than the intangible. A cycle. <u>A dialectical materialism that proceeds down to each subsequent generation through the ages</u>.

In the course of childhood one gradually learns the physical limits of his extension in each present moment of time and space. The limits of that extension located at the outer perimeter of his finger-tips and the bottom of his feet, as it were. And artificially extendable to the tip of his walking stick, or the contact between the tires of his automobile to the surface of the road.

The potential infantile mind comes into the world fitted up with brain or CNS which contains the necessary billions of neurons. However, a mere collection of an abundance of unconnected neurons does not constitute a mind; just as a mere dictionary of words does not constitute either a poem or a story. It is primarily the life experience and nurturing of the infant brain that stimulates an ever expanding <u>connections of neurons</u> of the infant brain to one another that begins the process of evolving those ever increasingly connected neurons into an active network of communication. <u>A tangible connection of neurons that correlates with mental conceptual connections. That is what eventually ends up producing the entity-which we call the intangible mind</u>. A network of interconnected neurons. A juvenile mind, that requires ever more connectivity, organization, and maturation into its functional networks until it reaches it full maturity in the early twenty-some years of its life.

The formation of pers0onal memories must surely involve a similar transformation in the connectivity of the brain.

✻   ✻   ✻   ✻   ✻

To Learn

It has been discovered that "the brains of learning animals synthesize increased amounts of RNA and protein. And that drugs which prevent such synthesis, also block the ability to learn. Increased metabolic activity and changes in efficiency and number of contacts between the nerve cells in any circuit must both involve synthesis of protein. Though the template of the protein produced is derived ultimately from protein messengers of genetic DNA, it is not that code that contains the new personal memory. <u>The resulting change in the number and pattern of nerve connections is... the new memory</u>." What also one "must store are the DNA genetic instructions needed to allow any circuit to change, depending on its own activity, without specifying in advance which circuit will be involved. (stochastic) The ultimate chemical contribution to mind's memory <u>is</u> then the genetically programmed <u>ability to learn</u>." (p.113-114 Blakemore)

"The emergence of capacity to learn is the triumph of evolution." "Learning frees the individual from the dictates of his own double helix (i.e. reflexes and instinct). The productive power of learning and memory gives the individual immense survival value. Learning allows each animal to add a stock of personal secrets to its description of the probabilities of the world." (pp. 113-114 Blakemore)

The man who says "I am a fool' is no longer as foolish as he may have been. "As the happiness or real good of man consists in right action and right action can not be produced without right opinion, it behooves us, above all things in this world to take care that our opinions of things be according to the nature of things. The foundation of all virtue and happiness is in thinking rightly." (Ben Franklin)

"There has been a strong philosophical tradition that clear and distinct ideas directly intuited by the mind [i.e. needs no proof] can be trusted. Nevertheless, no one has yet provided a clear and distinct idea of what these clear and distinct ideas are." "Standards of what is intuitively obvious or needs no proof have been continually corrected and refined." (p. 208-209 Abel) Thus, intuition has been discredited and there are doubts about intuition as a basis for knowledge. One might well suppose that intuition could be oracle from the inscrutable churnings of the subconscious mind?

✳   ✳   ✳   ✳   ✳

Bergson "argued that biological evolution has favored the insect, which relies on reflex and instinct, at least as much as it has favored the human being who (often misguidedly) relies of reason. A person's romantic craving for insight at times confuses experience with knowledge." (p. 208 Abel)

Who was the first ape to notice that he wasn't an ape. Darwinian evolution and genetics do establish the continuity of all living things, and weakens the claim that human mental activities are unique in the animal world. Human genes are composed of the very substances DNA, RNA, and proteins that constitute the genes of all living entities-plant and animal. The argument (that human essence is discontinuous with the rest of nature) cannot withstand the contrary evidence of anatomy, comparative anatomy, paleontology, genetics, and embryology.

✳   ✳   ✳   ✳   ✳

Ponder These Matters

On Philosophy

Durant suggests that in her early centuries Philosophy was honored as the queen of all knowledge, but little by little her children (the sciences) have matured and stolen the spotlight, leaving mother Philosophy neglected and without gratitude.

Cosmology → astronomy and geology
Natural Philosophy → Biology and Physics
Philosophy of mind → Psychology

The real and crucial problems have escaped Philosophy. Problems of state became hunting grounds of petty politicians. Nothing remained to Philosophy but riddles of epistemology and academic dogmas of an ethics that had lost its influence on mankind.

(Epistemology = scholastic theory of knowledge)

Descartes' dualism may be partly to blame when he accepted Socrates' invention of 'the soul' as a non-material substance-but leaving us with no notion as to how an incorporeal spirit can act upon the molecular substance of the brain.

Berkeley cleverly suggested that matter did not exist-i.e. discarded the idea of materialism. But that was a mere hypothetical assertion that held no water. "Nothing exists for any mind but that which that mind perceives." A truism which is quite different than "nothing exists unless it is perceived." (p.4 Durant)

But there remains the question as to whether "the qualities and objects which we ascribe to the outside world may in part or largely belong to concepts of the mind that perceives them." says Durant (p.4)

Came next the assertion that the function of Philosophy is to serve as a critique of scientific method. Unable to convince of the unreality of matter, Philosophy sought to demonstrate the unreliability of science. A chance to show that reason is fallible and that science can be said to demonstrate only a probability rather than a certainty. A chance to grace the assertions of outdated Philosophy into decorative new wrappings of newly deceitful elegant phraseology for remarketing to a new generation.

Scholars, mistakenly rated as philosophers, (having been primarily theologians), "set the fashion of subordinating the search for truth to the promulgation of the faith", says Durant. And producing *summas* for the propaganda office of the Vatican. And even informed us of their view "that Philosophy is the chambermaid of the Theology."

"To what is the obscurity of Philosophy due, if not to its imperfect honesty. It is perhaps time to recognize that much of the darkness which encompasses modern thought is due to the elusiveness of truth and the intrusiveness of cosmic considerations (science)." says Durant.

The meanings of poets are obscure, but poets still come away with some honor. "Woman is obscure, but what man this side of decay in not lured into the everlasting enterprise of penetrating that obscurity and solving that mystery?" (p. 6 Durant)

When a man speaks romantically, he is harder to understand than when he tells the truth. "Only an expert can make his mendacity seem as consistent as the truth. But experts in mendacity do no not become philosophers. They are too urgently needed in diplomacy" and politics. (p. 7 Durant)

✳ ✳ ✳ ✳ ✳

Philosophical Materialism

Darwin believed in and feared to expose something he perceived as far more heretical than evolution itself. Namely, <u>philosophical materialism</u>-the postulate that matter is the stuff of all existence and that all mental and spiritual phenomena are its by-products. In short, that mind is a product of brains. So says Stephen Jay Gould, in "Natural History" Magazine Dec 1974.

Recall that Darwin's formal education was intended to fit him up as a religious cleric. And that his extensive explorations into natural history led him to deductions and conclusions that were stoutly opposed by the religious establishment in which he had been educated. It might thus be said that his original religious bias did not determine nor taint his intention to honesty arrive at his theory of Evolution. Interestingly, and independently, Wallace (at about the same time) came to much the same conclusions as Darwin in his own explorations into natural history which were carried on in a different part of the world.

Both evolution and genetics would appear concerned <u>not</u> with any individual living creatures; but with Class, Genus, and species. (P. 115 Abel)

Phenomena such as mental images are <u>states of consciousness</u>. Characterized by their privacy and non-spatial nature. (i.e. not extensible) They include thoughts, belief, ideas, purposes, hopes, intentions, attitudes, wishes and memories. Also include such processes as attention, deliberation, expectation, anticipation, problem solving, awareness, perception, and preparation to respond. (p.197 Abel)

The progress of science in correlating or reducing mental states to physical states has weakened our confidence in the entity often designated as the intangible 'soul', or 'spirit'.

✳   ✳   ✳   ✳   ✳

Creationists Object

Those who champion the theory of Creationism appear perhaps mostly to be immersed in fundamentalist religion-which in itself suggests what motive lies at the foundation of those beliefs. From among this group emerges the notions of 'Intelligent Design' as antithesis to evolution. So called 'Intelligent Design' being suggested as a separate special and unique creation of our Homo sapiens species. Their theory to explain man's supposed endowment with 'soul'. A theory proposed to permit at least of some possibility for the 'theory' of evolution to have produced the other varieties of life.

Though there is nothing more than speculative evidence to support it, there remains also the unlikely possibility that mankind could have been transplanted among earth's life forms from some distant planet and civilization. Even if that were true, it does nothing to resolve the fundamental question of man's origin. And there exists abundant evidence to indicate that man is closely akin to "the beasts of the field" which we must suppose to be native to planet earth.

There are recent myths believed by many people concerning UFOs manned by aliens supposedly from other worlds. Also a large body of testimonials to support such claims, though as of yet, not enough of discovered evidence to substantiate any such claims. Certainly there exist interesting mega-structures such as pyramids at many places around the world; and drawings of immense scale of prehistoric origin etched onto earth's surface for which we have no certain explanation, as pointed our by Van Daniken for example. And we have two or three studied and well written books by Velikovsky on the 'catastrophic theory' of ancient geology and history that might capture one's imagination as to plausibility. It does appear that catastrophic events have punctuated earth's more gradual geological evolution and are probably responsible for the extinction of vast numbers of life species which we come to know of through the fossil discoveries of Paleontology. Indeed, evidences aplenty at least to suggest such things as visitations from other worlds, or very ancient highly technological civilizations that might once have existed on our planet. But we are well advised not to read too much into implausible hypothetical theories just because we do not as yet have definitive explanation concerning these many things from out of recent and prehistoric times.

✳   ✳   ✳   ✳   ✳

Cartesian Dualism or Dichotomy?

Descartes' Dualism proposed that mind and matter are equally fundamental, entirely independent, and mutually irreducible. How then does the will or intent of one's 'inner man' move my limb? (p. 200 Abel) How do we account for the interaction between what is non-spatial in nature, and what is spatial; between what is non-material and what is material? (p 199 Abel)

Dichotomy Rather Than Dualism?

And yet there does appear to be a dualism (in a non-Cartesian sense) with which we each must deal. For clarity, let us call it a 'dichotomy' rather then a duality. It concerns our conception of the world and universe outside of ourselves. For the (function of) mind is always subject to the illusions and misperceptions of our limited sensory mechanisms. Always a bit of dichotomy between what 'seems to be' and reality. A dichotomy with which we mere mortals each are continuously taxed to grasp and deal with in our limited mortal capacity.

Only some of that outside world and some of its qualities can our senses perceive directly by combining the information which is fed to the CNS by man's various separate senses. There is a considerable much that we are left to infer on the basis of our experience in the reality of that outside world. The analytic mind and its rational capacity does facilitate and extend the limits of our senses with the building of tools that are able to detect qualities within the world and universe that are beyond the capability of our natural unaided sensory capacity; and to transmit such additional information to our senses with magnification, amplification, and translation via things such as oscilloscopes. And devices such as infra-red cameras that can detect and translate to us another fraction of that very large electromagnetic spectrum to which we mere mortals are otherwise blind and deaf.

Thus scientifically provided with much expanded sources of information we are enabled to infer considerably more; and become ever more capable of testing, correcting, and verifying our hypotheses of the nature of "that-which-is". The spoken language and the written word in generation after generation of mankind permits and encourages us to grasp and deal with ever more; and ever more accurate information as mankind proceeds to probe ever deeper into the vast and mysterious unknown. The disadvantage of the brevity of our individual lives is thereby at least partially obviated.

The Cartesian myth also implies that in consciousness, self-consciousness, and introspection one is directly and authentically apprised of the present states and operations of his own mind. Still, there is some variation of opinion among the dualists as to whether a person does or can directly monitor all, or only some of his private history and the workings of his own mind.

The whole idea of a privileged access to one's own mind is confused. The angry man is often less aware of his own anger than are those who observe him. We are not always the best judges of our own states of consciousness. We fear self-knowledge because it is so often bad news. States of my mind such as remembering, knowing etc. must, like belief, be justified by appropriate action. The criterion for the existence of my internal mental capacity is its appropriate external exercise.

The workings of the mind are visible for example in the silent actions of a child at play. This is because many of the operations of the mind are 'dispositions'. Like solubility as an example-a disposition for sugar to dissolve in water. Now, knowing or believing etc. are dispositions in exactly this sense. For to say that a man "knows" something is to say, in effect, that under certain conditions (say, a test) he is able to give a performance of a certain kind. "Thus knowing is not a secret operation of a hidden entity but the observable exercise of a capacity and thus the view that the mind is some internal, mysterious ghost-like substance is false." (p. 185 Popkin)

But were things in accordance with the Cartesian doctrine, we would encounter then the insurmountable difficulty of explaining-the how of communication between the neurons of a tangible CNS and an intangible mind. What would be the interface between the tangible and the Cartesian intangible being. How possibly could the will and intention of the Cartesian supposedly intangible 'inner-man' execute its intentions of action onto the physical body? For that supposed interface connection can not be inspected either by introspection nor by experimentation.

And would not that any such 'inner-man' also be required to have a-mind-of-its-own? Which leaves one then once again faced with the infinite regression problem.

The reality, however, is that the mind is but a function of the brain tissue. And when that brain tissue along with the rest of the body dies, that function (mind of mortal man) ceases to exist.

On the one hand, 'minds' are <u>not</u> in space nor are their operations subject to mechanical laws. Nor can the workings of the unspoken private mind be directly witnessed by public observers. Only the individual being can take direct cognizance of the states of one's own mind and the workings thereof.

On the other hand the body, existing in space-time is subject to laws which govern all other bodies in space. And a person's bodily life is as much a public affair and subject to public inspection as are the lives of animals and, plants, crystals, and planets.

> The outer from the inner
> Derives it magnitude
> 'Tis duke, or dwarf
> As is the inner mood
> Emily Dickinson

Again, it is a necessary feature of the material body that it exist in time and space. But it is a necessary feature of mind that it exist in time-but <u>not</u> in space. It is absurd to hypothesize that mind-which does not exist in space-is yet then to be localized inside the skull as being an entity separate and apart from the CNS. Mind is a concept and function of neuronal tissue. Being merely a function of the CNS, it needs must co-exist only as nothing more than a function of CNS.

"It is not that every human being <u>has</u> a body and a mind, but rather that every human being <u>is</u> a body and a mind." (p. 23 Ryle) A CNS which houses a mind as one of its functions ('f of CNS'). Thus, each person is a Monism. Not a Cartesian dualism of individual man.

✳ ✳ ✳ ✳ ✳

Non-Cartesian Mind

Russell and Whitehead in *Principia Mathematica* (in the 1920's) proved that mathematics is a part of the subject of Logic-not a separate discipline. And that everyday natural languages such as English have a basic structure similar to that of *Principia Mathematica*. But that these natural languages are defective for purposes of philosophical analysis, since they are less precise. (p.178 Popkin) This then leads us directly to the works of Wittgenstein and one of his students, Gilbert Ryle.

Gilbert Ryle begins his commentary and analysis by pointing out that a myth is not necessarily a fairytale. Rather, it may be the presentation of the facts of one category which are presented in the idioms of another. An idiom being an expression different from the actual sum of the individual words of the expression. I.e. to say "take heart" which has an actual meaning of "take courage". He explains that to explode a myth is not necessarily to deny the facts, but to re-allocate them.

The subject of Ryle's book is a theory of mind, although the book gives no new information about minds-of which we already have considerable information.

Ryle presents to us a theory of mind from which the Cartesian myth is dispelled. He challenges the classical distinction between 'mind' and 'matter' which has haunted philosophy and psychology since the time of Descartes. The Cartesian Doctrine implies that a person lives through two collateral histories, one consisting of what happens in and to his body: the other consisting of what happens in and to his mind. Descartes' conception is that of a human 'duality' (i.e. independence of man's mind from one's flesh-and-blood). A duality which posits two separate components to the nature of man. One being immortal intangible mind; and the other being mortal tangible matter, including flesh and blood. And posits that neither can be reduced to the other. The problem then is to explain how mind and matter can ever influence or affect one another, since there is no evidence of an 'inner man' or 'soul' conjoined to man's tangible mortal being.

Dualism Implies also that after the death of the body, the mind (in other idioms called spirit or soul) may continue to exist and function. A misconception in that one's mind, thought, and consciousness exist only in consequence of the normal neuronal metabolic function of the wakeful brain. Mind is not something more than what can be produced by the physical anatomy and physiology of the CNS. It is but a function of brain and its neurons.

The reality is that the intangible conceptual mind and the tangible brain are but two separate aspects of the solitary CNS. One aspect is the anatomy and physiology of the brain and its neurons: and the other, a function of that anatomy and it's physiology. CNS functions which we conceptually consolidate into a conscious 'mind'. A mind which has the capacity to concern itself with the realization of intangible abstract possibility in conceptual thought. A mind which becomes the foundation of one's consciousness. Or might be thought of as the "machinery" of conscious and subconscious thought. A mind which is not a separate entity from flesh and blood, but only a function thereof.

Not therefore a 'duality' in the Cartesian sense of the word. Only yet a 'monad'. And so we human creatures have a conscious 'being' as well as a mere 'existence'-in that we function and respond not only to the tangible of our real world, but are enabled also to deal with that which is merely conceptual and such intangibles as mind, consciousness, possibility, time, value, quality, beauty, math, philosophy, etc. A welding or <u>unification of the intangible to the tangible</u>.

Yes, my own perceptions, experience, and understanding of the world and universe in which we have our being leads me to suppose that we mere mortals are each a monad with an ability to contemplate of both the tangible and the intangible. That <u>the function of the brain (flesh and blood) permits of a regular reciprocity of commerce between that which is 'the flesh and blood physical' and the mind's (conceptual) aspect of our human being</u>.

The evidence of that is straightforward. Man translates the mere idea of a telephone, into the actual invention of a telephone. From the abstract to the tangibly real. Or the other way around. A man sees a couple of tree trunks floating in a river. A stimulus that puts the conceptual idea of two logs together into the intangible mind, where the concepts are manipulated to bring forth the idea of more than two logs lashed together (a raft). From the real world, an abstraction is conceived into the intangible mind.

✳   ✳   ✳   ✳   ✳

It is Ryle's view that in the theory of knowledge of the great epistemologist's (Locke, Hume, and Kant), they "were in the main, advancing 'the grammar' of science when they thought they were discussing parts of the occult life-story of persons acquiring new knowledge. They were discussing the credentials of sorts of theories, but they were doing this in para-physiologic allegories." (p. 318 Ryle) That is to say in <u>postulating the existence of an intangible being within the skull</u> that in some inexplicable manner was thought to be able to transmit its will and volitions to activate the physical functions of life of the CNS in order to bring the body into action.

Abandonment of the Cartesian dualistic theory involves now a concomitant abandonment of the idea of a locked door to the inner core of the <u>previously assumed</u> private world of each person. An end now to the postulate that the human being has two lives running simultaneously. An end to the notion of each person possessing both a physical body and the postulated invisible inner "ghost" with its supposed and separate immortal life. An end to the notion of a somehow hidden inner life.

And thus, the search of Psychology for a key to a separate inner life has never been discovered. A 'promise' upon which they were never able to deliver.

We can easily accept though, that each person (himself alone) is witness to his own inner dialog as a part of his wakeful consciousness.

✳　✳　✳　✳　✳

Cause For Action

We are well advised to make a clean break and clarify our new awareness to be now free from the Cartesian dualist dogma which for so many centuries has muddled our concepts of the nature of reality of the truth of our existence. Notions of 'the-ghost-in-the-machine' can now be abandoned. Henceforth to designate the previously postulated notions of that ghost rather (instead), to be functions of the CNS. A function we call 'mind'.

We do not live two lives inside of our one head as the Cartesian dualists were wont to hypothesize. All of these things we call consciousness, sub-consciousness, and the perception of what we call our each individual life are intrinsic functions of the CNS.

We have become aware that our every muscular twitch and movement has its point of origin in the CNS. Which is to say it is mechanistic. A biological machine which encompasses the many functions that drive our embodied lives.

In the absence then of this (Cartesian) supposedly second inner being (soul or spirit); what is there then within or without that decides our actions and behavior? What and from whence cometh the guidance that directs us through this continuous and endless dilemma and necessity of decisions... of what it is that we call our lives? Combinations of the following:

- The calls of nature for food, water, air, and excretion regularly motivate us to action.
- Reflexes, somatic and autonomic.
- Instincts.
- Habits are acts that become largely automatic.
- Noise.
- Pain or Excessive heat or cold (physical discomforts)
- Personal interests, curiosity.
- Opportunity to self interests.
- Agendas.
- Vanity and indolence are also dispositional, but a disposition alone, is not a cause.
- Inclinations and curiosity.
- Under compulsion and expectation of family and tribe, or those to whom one must give an accounting.
- Urgings and demands of our milieu and society.
- Ordered or instructed to act by an authoritarian figure.
- A tendency or predisposition.
- Temporary moods or inclinations dominate over tendencies while they are in operation.
- Tenacity of character-Self control as a character strength.
- Propensity such as strength of resolve.
- Customs.
- Belief-a motive and disposition.
- Emotions and feelings i.e. passionate love and passionate hate.
- Agitations include: to be anxious, startled, shocked, excited, convulsed, flabbergasted, in suspense, flurried, and irritated.
- Motives presuppose to agitations.
- Perceptions of bodily threat and danger.

❊   ❊   ❊   ❊   ❊

Though our every move be governed by our conceptual and physiological laws, not one of them is ordained by those laws to happen. And while rules as in a game of chess are unalterable, the games are not uniform. A matter that speaks to the concept of free will.

"It is false to say that in life, circumstances decide. On the contrary. Circumstances are the dilemma, constantly renewed, in the presence of which we have to make our decision. What actually decides is our character [habits and predispositions]." (Ortega y Gasset)

There are distinctions between capacities and tendencies; distinction between knowledge and belief. Know is a capacity verb as well as a skill word. Skills have methods. Believe is a tendency or inclination verb as well as a motive word. We ask <u>how</u> a person knows this or that, and we anticipate a response such as will point to evidence. But we ask only <u>why</u> a person believes a thing.

"Beliefs, like habits can be inveterate, slipped into and given up. Like partisanships, devotions, and hopes, they can be blind and obsessing. Like aversions and phobias they can be unacknowledged. Like fashions and tastes they can be contagious. Like loyalties and animosities, they can be induced by tricks." (p. 134 Ryle)

The intent to know, on the other hand "is to be equipped to get something right" and to tenaciously apply one's skill in pursuit of that objective." (p. 134 Ryle) To know 'that' is of lesser quality of knowing than is knowing how to apply what one knows.

Dreaming Up Utopia

Trust in Government?

The shape of things is seldom so clear to those who live them in the here and now, as it might seem in retrospect. Thoughtful men have generally viewed their own times as times of confusion. But human nature continues to be much as it has always been. We mere mortals have been forever vexed with anxiety and always things to worry about. Our own times are not an exception to this. 'Pie-in-the-sky' and delusions of the always eminent 'peace-in-our-times' as promised again recently by Obama and his administrative clique is belatedly being seen as wishful thinking. Surely, even these perpetrators of the new Utopia are having to acknowledge at least to themselves that the vague hope and change of their rhetoric has been a great deal more of a failure than they could have anticipated. There is a rather catastrophic loss of confidence in the ever more partisan congress as well as in the Obama administration. Loss of confidence in politicians in general, in consequence of the seemingly endless string of political scandal and ongoing 'investigations' which are so much obstructed by conspiratorial bureaucrats that those guilty are forever able to elude the consequences of their public and personal misbehavior with and easy mendacity and 'plausible deniability'. They have become experts in political correctness and double-talk. Our government in becoming ever more sizable and so much increasingly complex that it begins to become un-manageable. It begins to become obvious that finally "we must learn navigation, or go on the rocks".

Prior to the 20th century man lived in a relatively sparsely settled world where he was neither powerful enough nor in sufficiently close continuous contact with his neighbors to do them or himself any much of all-encompassing fatal harm. Not so now.

Do the beliefs of mankind influence the course of events? We begin to see that they obviously do. Will mankind eventually begin critically to examine their beliefs? Will mankind ever be well enough behaved or capable enough of being educated so as to survive his capacity for self-destruction?

Is man's behavior totally determined genetically like that of the ant? Or at the other extreme is his behavior so much capable of influence by his social environment that he can be manipulated (by social scientists and supposedly well-meaning politicians) by unrealistic promises of perfecting the environment to fit man for some vague utopia of perfectly correct behavior, thought, and speech; and perfect equality in all things?

Or does man have 'free will' as a part of his human and all-significant consciousness? If that be so, then such other intangible qualities as noble character, beliefs, and values are matters of significance in his civilized milieu. What influential principles shall guide him-given the necessity of forever facing decisions and dilemma in the course of his daily life?

✳　✳　✳　✳　✳

The Grand Scheme

Before one and a half millennia ago, the Christian's Word-of-God and man's conscience were considered to be the mainstay of guidance to man of the western world through his moral dilemmas. But then Hobbs suggested that "the mind of man at birth was not a 'tabla ransa', but that it had been endowed with some vague principles of nature"- something outside of himself which he might stumblingly follow. In the 18th century, the hypothesis of <u>Evolution</u> lent at least some support to that. The <u>Marxist</u> hypothesis suggested that a historical dialectic from age to age was a part of the guiding principles *that* did and does gradually influence mankind and the course of human history.

And there came then from Freud and Jung, the notions of newly proposed Psychology-reinforced by Pavlov and Skinner. 'Conditioned reflex behavior'. The idea that psychological conditioning might be used to guide and direct man; and possibly fit each well-conditioned human being for living in some version of a perfect utopia. These three notions (of Evolution, of Marx, and of Psychology) drifted through the years into an assumption that we 'creatures-of-an-hour' "cannot, nor need not do much of anything for ourselves." That 'natural selection' would accumulate to us some positive traits such as might replace the necessity of personal aspiration and accomplishment. And with the arrival of our awareness of the (concept of) subconscious mind, we need not even aspire to follow the ancient injunction of 'know thyself'. Even secular Calvinism absolves us of any hint of personal responsibility in the face of unmovable predestination. Thus freed of the notion of personal responsibility, persons could begin to see themselves as victims. Exculpation. Not personally responsible for one's own misbehavior, errors, sins, or follies.

Like all "dogmas, these three do not have to be accepted in full rigidly in order to have a powerful effect" on individuals and populations. "Educators, Sociologists and Lawmakers have begun to suppose and act as if men were absolutely incapable of any choice, self-determination, or autonomous activity. Being treated as though man could do nothing for himself," we might suppose that men are likely then to begin to display less personal initiative and capability. "Especially when those capacities are ever less rewarded, or even tolerated." Politicians, misled by the exaggerated claims of Sociology and Psychology, begin to promise to achieve 'scientifically' all that which religion and moral Philosophy have failed to accomplish. Hence cometh the political 'progressives' along with the minions of the Obama administration. The whole broad 'benevolent effort' of social reformers to relieve poverty, provide opportunities for education, and remove as far as possible all corrupting features from the environment in which the individual grows to maturity. A fanatical contention that man is "nothing but" the product of his environment.

And the same fanatical conviction that man is limitlessly plastic to political manipulations which are intended to ready mankind for some inevitable new Utopia. Never mind that the long past history of a plethora of previous utopias have all proven to be abject failures. Nor can the political reformers eliminate (nor even hope to enumerate) the sum total of 'all' factors that are influential in the development of human character. Our human limitations are such that our processes of thought do not correspond to it sufficiently to permit us to think about it at all well." "Forever stopped from pushing our inquiries, not necessarily by the construction of the world, but perhaps by the construction of ourselves. Even the volunteers to all previous utopias seem historically to have become sickened of the business and made their escape or retreat, when that has been possible. Of the non-volunteers forced into the utopias, some 10 or 20 percent are usually pragmatically sought out and 'eliminated' by the political gurus even before the gates of Utopia are closed upon the thoughtless 'malleable masses'. [Reference Hitler's Germany, Stalin's USSR, Pol Pot's Cambodia, Mao's China.]

The mildest and most defensible of this fanatical conviction and benevolent effort is to be found in the hopes and efforts of social reformers to relieve and provide opportunities and remove all corrupting features from the environment. Their justifications depend on nothing more than a recognition of external influences as 'a factor' in determining human fate. And they seem not to demand for their justification any affirmation that human conduct or character is nothing but the product of the influences brought to bear upon the individual.

This human engineering business merely supposes of their being able to both predict and control human behavior. Predictable to some small degree on influence on the masses in the moving of merchandise. But expendable income is always ready to pursue tangible nonsense.

But there has been not much evidence to suggest that the mass of mankind is readily controllable or manageable, as one can see from the always and inevitable reality of ongoing protests, revolution, and warfare. Controversies in the minds of men inevitably arise to disrupt organizations and pit their internal factions against one another. What reason be there to suppose that will change?

Yes, some of the waywardness in children and in adults is partly attributable to what has been done to them; but always and entirely thus explicable? Ideas inevitably clash. And as such, these clashes continue to arise anew. A part of the character of the citizen.

Societies at times are partly the cause of some crimes, especially as when society makes new laws that are out of step with the common temper and tradition. And when the economic interests of one group are seen or perceived as overtly discriminatory. The toleration of inequities has always its limitations, both as to individual men and societies of men as a whole.

A Robinson Crusoe alone on his private island could never be guilty of any crime, because as living without the benefit of society his behavior could not be considered either social or antisocial.

Human infants are generally accorded a period of sustaining uncritical love even in their misbehavior. Gradually however each must be 'civilized' by being exposed to a guiding criticism and discipline. Parents (and the prevailing society to which the infant is exposed) who fail adequately to tame the child's narcissistic 'id', and exaggerated 'ego' eventually then release even the wayward and overly aggressive adult offspring into society. But even when properly tamed to function compatibly within society, the self-serving id and self-righteous superego remains able to oppose the overly ambitions designs of social reformers. That tendency is a part of what we call the character of the individual, and is always to some variable degree influential as to how far one's conscious person will permit itself to be manipulated, taxed, and suppressed. Under the strain of brain-washing, the naked id and inflated superego will perhaps submit to yet just a bit more of 'conditioning', but always at the price of leaving a bit more perhaps of tension within the individual psyche. Making it the more ready at some point to 'snap' and revolt. Good-by then to the ever new version of Utopia.

✳   ✳   ✳   ✳   ✳

The Process

How can a man be in some sense responsible for what he does without being free to do anything else? In its contest with the world, the id/ego of a person can expand with various hatreds, resentments, and evil desires. There within the id/ego, they can remain, inscrutable, and only tenuously suppressed by one's superego from making their way into the active and functioning invisible id/ego.

The creative dreamers of utopias needs must come to recognize that their any hope for a viable utopia implies changes in both man and society that are far more radical than any assumed or even desired by the mere reformist. In order to be a fit candidate for induction into a viable utopia, the individual must not only be willing to submit to 'conditioning'. He but he must be conditioned willingly to like being conditioned. That is not the nature of the individual man, which always clings desperately and uncharitably to its own private self-serving interests. The powers of reason and the ego have but little of influence within the realm of the inscrutable private agenda. Ego and superego are both influenced and fed by the always self-serving id which is the fundamental animal nature of man (and all sentient creatures).

Our life in the work-a-day world continuously informs us that it is well always to be suspicious of even those closest to our persons. And far more dubious of what does and ought to transpire even in our own small immediate society. Suspicious especially of foreign societies, and of our own social reformers and politicians. All, seem forever to manifest their own <u>private agendas</u>-which we read and hear about every day. Disgusting and ongoing.

What are the details and how well thought-out are the plans, intentions, and purposes of the social reformers and politicians? We of the masses are to be acted upon by our egotistical 'managing' leaders who <u>present themselves</u> and their plans <u>as benevolent</u> on our behalf. Take a look at what goes on even publicly in the white house, congress, and the halls of justice. Only occasionally do we get a glimpse of then the even darker <u>mischief behind</u> their <u>closed doors</u>. Consider even just for example the recently enacted "Affordable Care Act". It is obvious that even those who submit and vote it into law have not even read (let alone comprehended) the details (let alone the consequences) of what we tax payers have now been saddled with.

Keep in mind then that those who conceive and advocate for their various utopias are of the same stripe as your current 'legislators and administrators'. They too expect to be 'at the helm' of the New Utopia with special prerogatives, special status, and ongoing 'authority'. Always necessarily in the process of "winging it", since they are never so able to predict behavior and eventualities as what they are wont to presume and proclaim. Historically, the outcomes have not been good. Rather, and commonly, evil in their consequences. Think of Russia under Lenin and Stalin. Think of Germany under Hitler. Think of Cambodia under Pol Pot. Think of Jim Jones in Guiana. And in considering these examples we must acknowledge the reality that is already all too evident. That many (if not all) of the individuals of any particular group may be made to act and think in ways which we would once have thought inconceivable. Think of the current situation concerning jihad and ISIS among Muslims. Even the democracy under which we live does not inevitably safeguard us against the arbitrary use of power. As to the authority behind our government, we do well to keep in mind that "there can be no possible reason for taking a vote if the results can either be determined or even predicted in advance."

Keep in mind that every mortal being has his own private agenda, regardless how ill-formed and naïve. Man is more than the product of society. Always somewhat the product of himself. Yes, "the child too, is father of the man."

❋   ❋   ❋   ❋   ❋

Idols Of The Laboratory

Could it be said that we regard material goods as the only real goods and that increase in wealth and comfort is the only end worth pursuing? A materialistic Philosophy. But just because we have learned effective methods toward such ends does not necessarily mean we pursue no other goals and achievements. The means by which one achieves one's goals may or may not speak to the question of whether we have or have not some esthetic ideals, such as values, sense of balance and proportion, good taste, and appreciation of beauty. Can it be said that one and all are charitable of heart and are beings of essentially good-will towards one's fellow mortals? What is moral vs. what is evil; what is good vs. what is bad? Public criticism and self criticism would seem to be ever essential in maintaining a due regard for such intangibles as these. Do we have and take time for such considerations? Does the obvious of material plentitude simply speak more eloquently and obviously than do the vague intangibles of individuals and the hypothetical mentality of an entire society?

Anthropologists who study past and present societies of mankind note that there is considerable variation from one society to another as to what is moral vs. immoral, good vs. bad, honorable vs. dishonorable etc. There seems also to be considerable variation of opinion concerning such things among even individuals of current civilizations and societies in our very own times. And in our busy lives and societies, who among those beings takes or can find time to much ponder such matters? Mostly the 'professionals' who make their living out of these endless speculations and by preaching and writing books and essays on such matters. And by teachers who touch on such matters as a part of the school curriculum. And as to those who study and advocate a sort of scientific morality, they often make little distinction between what men do vs. what man ought to do. Commonly take polls by questionnaires, and are wont to suggest that what is predominant among responses is perhaps that which is most correct, as in the Kinsey study concerning sexual behavior in our times. "Turning the quest for morality into a study of what is prevalent."

The often cited "self-evident" in morals and values are be no means seen as such by all. Not uncommonly mere assertion in attempt to validate a line of their argument. Is that which has long survival the ultimate test of worth in a society or individual? Not all agree that the longest-lived men are the best.

The crocodiles are said to have been said to have inhabited this earth a goodly number of millions years and can be said to have worked out very satisfactory strategy, but has their philosophy of survival been of any value itself?

✳   ✳   ✳   ✳   ✳

The Minimal Man

There appears to be a middle ground between an **idealism** which asserts that 'mind' plays the only decisive role in the shaping of history on the one hand; while on the other hand there is a materialism which sees the universe as affected by nothing except 'things'. Only a very small sector of the public concerns or is even aware of such philosophical concerns.

The argument has a long history, the main question being: <u>to what extent man may hope to make free choices</u>. <u>To be responsible for his own conduct</u>. To make, rather than to have imposed upon him, value judgments. Do we have 'free will' and are we "the captains of our souls". Skinner's behaviorism school of psychology is among the foremost voices suggesting that our every mortal thought and act is imposed upon us by the combined genetic influence and the multiple environmental factors and influence under which we are raised from our infancy. If that be the case, then, no matter what be our mistakes nor however heinous be our crimes, we cannot truly be said to responsible for them.

The Philosophers, Sociologists, and Psychologists who lean towards the ideas of Skinner are wont to drift in among and become included (or at least supportive) with the various schemes of our social reformers. To them, all crimes and antisocial behaviors seem to be theoretically correctable if only once we can manage to create a utopia where all persons think and act kindly and respectfully of one another. Where none would ever have to suffer from want of the material necessities of life, nor have cause to envy one another, as there would be full equality of ready access to an always adequate availability of material goods. Where all would willingly and fully cooperate in 'the program' and efforts of utopia to assure that the necessities of life would be always forthcoming and available. In short, a sort of heaven on earth. Except of course, that all would needs must exert themselves to sustain the good life in utopia. And contribute fully of themselves in the effort. For it is only unceasing cooperative production (not vague 'good-will') that would be capable of supplying our unceasing necessities and wishful desires. Will individuals of sloth; and will private agendas cease ever to exist?

Of course the social reformers are realistic enough to see that there is little prospect for the immediate establishment of any such utopia now or in the immediate future. But they do have hopes and agendas to use their limited time and influence to sort of nudge society in the direction of utopia, step-by-step with incremental social action and gradual implementation of redistribution of wealth, and social governmental counseling to the individual, so as to temporarily soften and control crime and antisocial behavior.

But there are natural disparities among peoples and persons that would be difficult to obviate; and jealousies and envy account of it. White folks seem commonly to wish to be darker and thus need more exposure to the sun. Dark people tell us that black is beautiful, yet they tend to be envious of those among themselves who are a shade or two less colored than themselves. Tall people have always some advantage over short folks. Short folks also have advantages to be envied by the taller....

The psychic environment of the New Utopia would needs must have its existence based upon the reality that the natural man of our time is enough capable of being educated and enough malleable to make of him a fully predictable cog in the functioning of the 'new world order'. Capable of being educated out of his long established prejudices and incorrect beliefs. And even willing to want to submit to such psychological conditioning. Must be willing and able to believe that his mentors in this conditioning are well enough informed to know what is true and what is not true concerning the nature of man and of the universe.

How would people be educated to rid and assure that they have no counterproductive prejudicial beliefs to be a cause of discord? At our current crossroads of history it is plain to see that variation in beliefs is (and ever has been) an inevitable cause of strife and conflict. There appears to be a significant limit in the willingness of people to give up their religions and other deep prejudice. How will 'our masters of the utopian system' settle these differences to the satisfaction of all? Though the social engineers and psychologists are wont to assure us that they have "sometimes" had "some" successes as with advertising, propaganda programs, statistical predictions, and individual psychotherapy, yet they fail to acknowledge that even "often" is by no means "always". There is no reason for us to suppose that that they can create 'the minimal man' who is fit for survival in their new utopia. One 'can't create a silk purse out of a sow's ear". Nor can the social engineers foresee the consequences of the rules and regulations of the vague utopia of their imaginations. "Who has sight so keen and strong, that it can follow the flight of a song" (or a thought?) [*"Trees"* by Joyce Kilmer]

The individual man is also a part of the aggregate of mankind. Though much influenced by forces outside of himself and predictable on a statistical basis, the individual continues to be able to exercise an individual freedom. Needs must do so, in the face of the unpredictable circumstances to be faced regularly each day. "Who knows how large that area of freedom is? Or how influential the example I set may be; or within what limit's the behavior of the aggregate itself may be altered?" Even the atoms of what we call dead matter, do not, individually obey the statistical laws of determinism.

Ultimately, all that one has is his one life. One must presume that it has some value at least to oneself. If that be so, we needs must live and explore that life to determine what that value might be. That cannot be done unless we have some freedom to investigate. Freedom itself must therefore be a thing of value. One is immediately faced with the reality that the freedom which confronts one is very much limited. Like the chick in the shell, one must exert oneself to get free of that first constraint. And beyond that, there is ever always the next constraint to be faced and dealt with. Without one's necessarily realizing it, the constraints are at least of two sources. The limitations of one's own body and mind; and those imposed by his compatriots and the circumstances of the outside world. Happily we discover that the body and the mind grow. The nature of one's circumstances is such that one is subjected to discipline from the outside world, which also demands and encourages us in the matter of self-discipline. One's immediate family and community are a very significant determinant in one's gradual emergence into an adult status. But an even more potentially significant determinant in the evolution of one's being is the discovery within the self of one's own will and determination to shape and form his own character and abilities. Character, will, and abilities that are to be a significant determinant of opportunities and the pathways of life that will open onto him. The possibilities of what one might do and make of himself are abundant, but very much constrained by the limits of the span of each mortal life and one's circumstances of health and economic and social situation in life. And by fate.

One is confronted every day with the inevitable necessity of life's constraints and his interconnections of loyalty to those who constitute his family, friends, and social milieu. One must forever make choices as to his course and conduct each day. Choices which the individual must decide on the basis of values and goals in the limitations of always the immediate here and now. How then to proceed in this life of limited freedom, and the dilemmas of choice and values?

Yes, man is an animal, but few in our times would suggest as said Descartes, that, all animals "act naturally and by springs like a watch" or that all lesser animals "eat without pleasure, cry without pain, grow without knowing it, desire nothing, fear nothing, and know nothing".

＊　＊　＊　＊　＊

Stubborn Fact Of Consciousness

We mortal beings have choices and decisions to be made on a continuous basis and "free will opens the possibility of radical novelty in the universe." Says Wm James

Since Guttenberg's movable type arrived and the presses began to churn out words, ideas, and concepts (information) the doors were opened to ever more of a population of 'thinking man'. Dogmatism has had to contest with ever evolving scientific thought and philosophical ideation. A reality of which one ought be aware is that most philosophers are not religious; and that most theologians are not philosophers. Though the subjective world of delusions and dreams stubbornly persists, the renaissance of new thought and ideas has come to oppose that **subjective** with the **objective** world of new information and ideation backed by fresh observations and experimental evidence.

Science has come to be divided into the hard sciences such as Chemistry, Biology, and Physics, as opposed to the soft sciences such as Psychology, Sociology, and Political Science. And somewhere in between them remains an intermediate domain of Mathematics and Secular Philosophy which make themselves useful as tools to both the hard sciences and the soft sciences.

Notions of utopianism were hatched within a framework of religious dogmatism in the form of monasticism and the clergy. A great many of such utopian arrangements have had their day and their influence historically, only to fall short of their intent and come to failure. The planning and formation of such is abundant in even the short history of our own nation. Many such are hatched anew and still with us. Now from the soft sciences, notions and schemes of ever new utopias have continued. Skinner's book, *Walden Two* represents his notions as to how such another Utopia might be organized and come into being (scientifically). That, based upon his study and experimentation with 'the conditioned reflex'.

The general notions of utopias as proposed to those who might volunteer to join them is that of a sort of social and economic equality between its members and some probable basis of economic sustainability based on production and a sharing of the work load to make that happen. Based simultaneously upon some sort of religious or philosophical commonality of its members. The founding of most utopian groups occurs within an extant nation and society which is already functioning, and which is already based on its own principles and ideals. The new utopia then withdrawing into its own private community and properties and the pooling of the assets of its individual subscribers. Their mysticism is based upon the assumption that one can quit the game. And their Socialism is based on the notion that each one can break even. Capitalism on the other hand is based upon the assumption that one can win-and some do. Still, it can hardly be denied that Big Money and Big Corporate business practices in cahoots with increasing government malfunction have managed to distort pure capitalism and rig that game against the common man in our times.

As with founding of communistic government, the general plan for the New Utopia is that there be an elite and enlightened leadership to organize and administer the new political-economic entity. But that there then shall gradually come into existence a new society of perfect equality and economic plenty. But that, only after the necessity of a great struggle to tame and control the masses of members with enlightened thought and training in civil deportment. The volunteers to such schemes must subscribe to the belief that the organizers and leaders are honest and have benevolent intentions-naïve assumptions. And that there is significant workable validity in the scheme of operation. The success of their community will depend on their ability to produce from scratch, an economically viable community to be carved out of some wilderness by dint of hard work and the enterprising individual efforts of each member of the community.

But overlooked is the reality that their 'leaders' and the individual constituent members, like themselves, have each their counter-productive private agendas.

The latest variety of Skinnerite social engineers have noted that the body seems to function very like a machine, and are want then to suppose that the human mind can similarly be manipulated mechanically by reflex conditioning as they demonstrate in a rat or other experimental animal in the laboratory. That would seem to be true to some degree. Yet there would seem to be a self-serving awareness within each person that is resistive to any totality of conditioning. That of which we each are most aware, is a conscious awareness of self and a will of self-serving-interest. That consciousness would seem to be the major characteristic of the mind, which is an intangible consequence of the functioning CNS. Something perhaps the nature of an electrical field, but that in some fashion has a reciprocity of effect such as to enable it to use the functioning brain as I am now using my word processor. An autonomous power of thought. Consciousness is in fact **the primary thing** of which we adult mortals have direct evidence-when we get around to noticing it. All other input from the senses is mediated from the real world to our conscious being through the sense organs and CNS. "The consciousness that you and I perceive is constructed from the avalanche of sensations that pour into the wakened brain [from the external world, as well as from our own internal sensory-motor system]. Working at a furious pace, the brain summons up its memories to screen and make sense of the incoming chaos." Only a small part of that information is selected for higher-order processing. From that small part, small segments are enlisted through symbolic imagery to create the white-hot core of activity which we call the conscious mind." (p. 132 Wilson) "Though there be good reason for distinguishing the 'objective' reality of the world from the world of the 'subjective' mind, there is no justification for calling only the one real." (ibid p. 123)

The realm of conscious mind is not composed exclusively of sensations. In it there somehow exist also the emotions, pride, guilt, and shame. **So too is logic and discourse**. One might well suppose the autonomy of the human being likewise to be lodged within that intangible conscious mind. A consciousness that is active rather than a mere passive observer. Active, with a will to be and a will to know. Exploratory.

Before Darwin's time, the rationalists of the day were wont to call themselves 'Deists' rather than atheists or agnostics because they did not see how the universe of living things could simply have happened. Yet, evidence suggestive of design or pattern left them with nothing more than Lucretius' 'blind chance' by way of explanation. Darwin's 'natural selection' mechanism has now proposed an alternative explanation. A theory that has gradually become more conclusively established by a considerable body of new evidence as the sciences have matured.

The proposition of 'random mutations' within Darwin's theory still leaves us with the matter or chance and unpredictability. One might still argue that mind (universal or individual) could have been or has been a part of the cause, intention, or purpose behind this riddle of being. But on the other hand, the nature of things need not necessarily have any particular intention or purpose whatsoever. And the supposition of a Deistic mind still leaves us with then yet no explanation of the origin of Deity. Just a hypothetical interjection, leaving us with another unnecessary step to the seemingly unknowable cause of the matter, things, information, and energy that constitute our universe.

Does evolution by natural selection rob life of purpose? It might rather be said that evolution creates purpose. Generation after generation of evolving traits and potential to overcome the ever new threats and problems of life.

Evolution generates problems and solutions just as it generates life. Rocks may crack and erode, but they do not have problems. Amoebas and apes have problems. Purpose emerges slowly in the chain of life, in the species, and in the individual. Purpose pursues any direction provisionally more promising or more interesting than another. Like design, <u>purpose emerges rather than precedes</u>. Certain capacities have evolved repeatedly, because of the singular advantages they offer: senses, locomotion, minds, emotions, sociality, intelligence, creativity, and cooperation, to name those that concern us most. But still, evolution has no foresight. [see p. 259 Brian Boyd's essay, "Purpose-Driven Life" from *The American Scholar*]

Though consciousness and other manifestations of the mind seem to elude simple mechanistic explanation, they do exist. The senses transmit purely quantitative electro-chemical impulses to the brain. But from there they are translated into wholly different qualities of sensation in the mind. "The miracle of mind is that it can transmute <u>quantity</u> into <u>quality</u>. A thing that we needs must accept though we cannot explain." (p.131 Krutch)

"But mind is not an entity in its own right, and our conscious minds are not little separate creatures inhabiting our skulls", as Huxley puts it. But "'mental activity' has clearly been shown to be tied in with cerebral activity." A relationship that is far more intimate than religion would assume.

It would appear that natural selection (in maintaining and increasingly developing an ever higher degree of consciousness) has infinitely elaborated the most elusive aspects of consciousness (such as those which involve a conviction of autonomy and the making of value judgments which do not seem to be those of 'nature'). We must presume then some survival value in that.

In our investigation of the human mind, we must certainly study physiology, and material structure, and observable behavior. But unless we combine this with analysis, interpretation, and deduction, we shall not get very far, as the fate of the Behaviorist Psychology movement shows.

"Chemistry is older than life, and reflex action is an older characteristic of living things than is the power of conscious thought." (p. 135 Krutch) In the matter of conscious awareness, Homo sapiens appears to have that in common with even his nearest cousins among the great apes. It would appear to be the case that conscious human mind has already become an operative factor in the ongoing evolutionary process of man himself, as well as the world in which he exists. A consciousness finally enough advanced as to suggest an explanation as to why the reflex conditioning of Homo sapiens can never be as complete as the conditioning that is attainable in rats and there would seem to be a wide chasm of difference between laboratory animals.

Persistent Uncertainty

Old Fashioned Science Of Man

Pre-Renaissance man seemed as though "so certain as to the 'why' the Universe existed that they thought little to concern themselves with the 'how'." "(p.175) As though perhaps one wheel ran by faith, and the other by the grace of God. Dante put it all together for the deficit of imagination once 'the Holy Sea' had conjured up the notions of heaven and hell. Francis Bacon strove to encourage the investigative sciences; and Newton delivered the notions of gravity and the beginnings of a mechanistic view of the world. Animals and man too, came eventually to be seen as mechanistic. And eventually the social scientists and psychology began to view minds as of that same nature. Pavlov discovered the phenomenon of 'the conditioned reflex' which led some scholars to notions of 'behaviorism' and a sort of scientifically founded hope for the long sought-for Utopia by making human behavior predictable and obedient to the methods of social scientists.

There continues to be speculation as to whether the visible or the unseen spiritual world are at the root of the foundations of the universe, life, and our individual human existence. Freud and Jung contributed their speculations into the private internal psychic being of individual man. This speculative business of the human 'spirit' versus the 'soul' (invented by Socrates), versus the consciousness (of id, ego, and superego, conceptions postulated by Freud) were at the heart of man's private inscrutable mental life. Spirit, soul, and the above three components of consciousness-all, theoretical constructs. In either case, it must finally be recognized that there exists the intermediating function of the brain or CNS between one's private internal world of conscious awareness and the certainty of a shared but separate external world and universe.

In any case we come to accept a world which may not be precisely what it seems as well as operates largely outside of our consciousness.

We are each aware of the idea of an object (or of the world) as we experience it in our conscious intangible mind. But the actual details of material objects is partly inferred. These two realities (intangible idea, and tangible object) are qualitatively and absolutely distinct and seem to have their being in discontinuous realms. "The matter and energy of the universe seem to differ in much the same manner as do mind and brain." (p. 184)

Are matter and energy separate and distinct, or simply loosely interchangeable. A matter pointed to by Einstein with his E=M x C squared. "If that be so, then the distinction between <u>what is material and what is non-material can perhaps be regarded similarly</u>. And likewise, the dispute as to whether man be simply a machine or an intangible spirit, or perhaps both at one and the same time." (Krutch)

Its true that we do not know how the universe operates, where it is going, or its ultimate destiny.

And common sense offers us no insight into those mysteries

"When the modern view of the world began to take shape 300 years ago, it was the result of a revolt of common sense against everything that was repugnant to it. A declaration of <u>faith in the senses</u> as opposed to the speculative mind; <u>and in the visible world as opposed to the unseen</u>. But now faced again the realities of uncertainties (supported by quantum physics), we "once more live in a universe which is not at all what it seems-either to the senses or to common sense. What we think we see with our eyes or touch with our hands seems to us to exist in that form perhaps because our senses give us an inaccurate, or incomplete report of it. Again, always somewhat illusionary, as said by the ancient mystics." (p. 177 Krutch)

✳ ✳ ✳ ✳ ✳

The Function Of Discourse

Krutch indicates that the function of his current writing is <u>to raise doubts and reveal paradoxes</u>. Most of the emphasis has been on what we do not know, rather than on what we do know. And emphasis on the limitations of human understanding. But he makes no pretense that the validity of hypotheses other than the mechanistic has been definitely established. Has suggested that in some realm of human freedom man exists, that value judgments may have some ultimate meaning, that thought and preference may in some way be autonomous. And that all of this remains hypothetical.

If light behaves as though it were both a wave and corpuscular, the paradox is no less difficult to resolve than the paradox of man who seems both free and to some extent predictable by statistical methods. Hanging in the balance remains the question of whether our species is better served and more likely destined to come under totalitarianism versus democratic principles. Both make claim to having the best interests and welfare of the citizen at heart. The question remains confused. Despite the tendency to speak of democracy and totalitarianism as completely antithetical it is often very difficult to see any very sharp logical distinction between what is often meant by the one or the other.

Communism is wont to suggest that democratic principles of open discussion and voting are mere fetishes. To many among us in this nation there seems ever more to be some validity in that accusation. The wealth of the mighty and its economic force tempts and encourages the elected representatives to accept bribes rather than serve the best interests of the electorate and the nation. One might well make the case that the best form of government may well be one that is **for** the people-but not necessarily **of** the people, since the folks are unable or unwilling to elect politicians who are dedicated to serving the will of the electorate. (p. 202 Krutch)

That within us which is emotional, conceptual, and moral make almost as strong an impression upon one as do the sensory nerves upon one's CNS. The impression both of the sensory and the conceptual are a part of our being. And so we note again a direct relationship between our conceptual and tangible worlds.

"Body and mind are connected in some manner for which simple rationality has no name, and which is difficult for it to conceive. Perhaps there is some sort of psychosomatic relationship which exists, not merely within the human body, but in the universe at large. If the mind may produce effects on the body as surely as the condition of the body can affect the mind, why should it be difficult to believe that for example, a moral conviction may sometimes determine what will happen to a man just a surely as what has happened to his physical being may sometime determine what his moral conviction will be?' (Krutch p. 209)

"Whatever is real in the mind, is too real to be disregarded." (p. 243 Krutch) 'Man has always been partly the creator and partly the creature of his own environment." (p. 254 Krutch) "Human intelligence is weak, and the pressure of events is always forcing it to choose some method and some principle for dealing with its problems." (p. 257 Krutch)

✻　✻　✻　✻　✻

The Abacus And The Brain

"That we think-or rather that we are aware-is of all things, the one thing which we know most directly and incontrovertibly." (p. 165 Krutch) The most important as well as the most obvious fact about us.

"The abacus and the slide rule were both created by man," (p. 161) Many subsequent electronic devices are of the nature of being something akin to miraculous and can perform operations of mathematics and logic much more quickly and efficiently that can the human brain; just as the automobile, the train, and the airplane can move us about on the surface of the earth much quicker than can our limited appendages of locomotion. These inventions are very useful extensions to our limited human capacities, but they are the creations of human intellectual capacities and a tribute to the power of inventiveness of the human mind. It seems quite likely that human inventiveness will continue to create a great lot of what is yet unimaginable to us. Inventions that are certainly a tribute to the faculty of human imagination and intelligence. But they are not human beings, and one need not look for them to soon replace mortal man at or near the top of the food chain. Robots may seem to be docile and as much dedicated to the service of man as our pet animals are companionable, but they are potentially as malicious and dangerous to mankind and human civilizations as are we mortals to one another. When they are given license as agents to perform maliciously, will we be saying of them that they are evil. Or, as in the case of wild beasts, will they evade that designation?

It doesn't seem likely of course that robots will have cause to laugh or love, experience delight, enjoy music, or be curious or sympathize with anyone or anything. Will it have pretences or have beliefs?

But Life Goes On

Essence Of One's Being

We human beings live out our lives at once in both aspects of the reality of the world and universe in which we live. The physical and the metaphysical. Or if you prefer, call it the tangible and the intangible. Or the bodily and the conceptual. All other creatures besides ourselves abide there with us.

The advantage that we human beings have over all other species is that we have the gifts of language; and that we live out our lives in an ever advancing cultural tradition. Language and cultural advantage that enables us with the capability for a dialectic of advancing conceptualizing ability. With that advantage, we at last become aware of our own awakened consciousness-a mind. Enabled more clearly then to conceptualize into the previously inscrutable aspect of the intangible or metaphysical aspect of our human being. And of our place in the world and universe.

Our human advantage in the matter of powers of the mind and widening of consciousness evolves considerably from infancy to adulthood as body and brain mature. And our advantage above that of other species seems to correlate with our proportionately larger cerebral cortex. Certainly it is not unreasonable to suppose that cerebral cortex function generates mind and consciousness.

In recent years Astronomers have detected a strange new inscrutable something in the vast universe which they call dark matter and dark energy. A something which in some unaccountable manner appears to influence the laws of gravity. Might it be possible that this will turn out to be a manifestation of what may be called the mind of the universe?

Descartes' Dualism remains then as a historical concept of discussion in the literature of philosophy though we abandon its implication of the existence of a 'soul' or the immortal existence of an independently existing 'inner little man' which was previously said to survive one's physical death into another life in the hereafter. In the interests of clarity it is then best to abandon the notion of 'soul' and the postulate of Cartesian 'dualism'.

We have instead to deal with what we might best term the concept of the intangible 'mind', which is an immaterial aspect-or function of the CNS. A function which is an additional asset to one's genetically hard wired CNS reflexes and instincts. A function which supervises and often overrides the functions of reflexes and instinct.

An intangible mind which is the basis and essence of one's solitary private existence from the intangible realm of ideas; and yet a light unto one's ubiquitous inevitable dilemma and confrontation in the world of tangible reality. A mind in touch with the world and universe through the sensory systems of one's physical body which reports to the neurons of one's brain tissue. Neurons whose function is to then transmute that data into the realm of intangible conceptions of the intangible mind. A sensory system upon which the intangible mind is dependent even to be in touch with its own body. But, that (process of) mind does <u>not</u> survive beyond the death of the individual's brain and neurons which generate that process.

✳　✳　✳　✳　✳

Comportment of Self

How shall we comport ourselves in this business of our daily navigation through the social, political, and commercial aspects of a populous civilization?

Perhaps innately and undoubtedly reinforced within us by our familial and social upbringing, human beings are imbued with an inner sense of fairness and justice which we note within ourselves even often when we do not act or even speak out when we are witness to it. Dare we speak up to a bully or an authoritative figure? Some sense of fairness is reported even in the behavior of chimps, for example, by those who study them in the wild and in the laboratory.

Human intelligence is weak, yet the pressure of events in the course of a life is forever forcing one to choose some act, method, or principle for dealing with the problems of one's existence in the real world of one's being-and into which one is embodied. The artist might choose to depict as a halo of cloud-that which we might conceive of as the nature of the intangible mind. There abide the factors of what we may denote as focus of conscious attention. And patterns of self-constraint and 'permissible' behavior (superego and ego) which constitute our individual character and moral code. Character and moral code which from infancy grow, and solidify as components of the ever expanding conceptual 'mind'.

We hear it said that "Half at least of all morality is negative, and consists in keeping out of mischief." (p. 43 Huxley)

Here is another point of contention. I would argue (along with Ethan Allen) that reason is man's **only Oracle**. Others postulate that man also has a conscience. But then can we in fact clearly distinguish what we call 'conscience' from that 'inner sense of justice' as discussed previously? It certainly appears that 'conscience' is of variable intensity from one person to another. Very probably related to the degree in which it has been reinforced at mother's knee and general upbringing of a youth. And as with that inner sense of justice and fairness, 'the voice' of conscience often remains unspoken to the world.

And so it is well to be reminded of the <u>Silver Rule</u> from Confucius, "who gave the world not a philosophy, nor a creed, but a lofty moral code." (p. 353 Durant) The more idealistic <u>Golden Rule</u> has but limited application and only in limited circumstances ought one be tempted to apply it. Like the <u>Iron Rule</u>, it requires one's considered judgment in evaluation of the character of those of one's acquaintance.

One needs must consider the reality of the limitation of our physical extensibility, our time, our economic resources, and our energy of life. Therefore, in general, our interactions and physical ministrations are prudently centered upon kith and kin near at hand.

> The ways of shining heaven are far.
> Turn thou, ah turn,
> To things yet near.
> Turn to thy earthly home oh friend,
> And try to do thy duty here.
> Omi Okura

For the same reasons, and because even the bonds of kinship and friendship are not infrequently tainted by some animosities; therefore 'The Golden Rule' is not necessarily always applicable between one's self and even close family and friends-let alone all of mankind. The Silver Rule is generally much more widely applicable. And where one is confronted with definite animosity and malevolence, one must not flinch in the application of the 'Iron Rule'.

Well, who am I to judge the character of my fellow man(?), you will be asking yourself. And in reply, I remind you that both you and I make such judgments on a regular basis. This business of living in a crowded, complicated, and dangerous world requires that we do so. We must make our judgments and then apply one of the three great rules (the Golden Rule, the Silver Rule or the Iron Rule) to every person with whom we have dealings, every day. Yes, to everyone that we merely even only encounter, every day. Those judgments are not of the nature of an indictment, but rather, merely a cautionary routine approach to one's necessity of avoiding unnecessary dangers and un-pleasantries.

Now then, this brief summary of the three great rules. No one of them seems to me more useful than the others. Each has its own particular application and usefulness. We must apply one or another of them, to our relationships with all other people.

- The **Golden Rule**: Do onto others as you would have them do unto you. A fine objective of limited applicability.
- The **Silver Rule**: Do not do unto others what you would not have them do unto you (Live, and let live, when that be done without encountering open and aggressive hostilities).
- The **Iron Rule**: Do not permit others to do onto you, what you would not do unto them (Defensively enforcing the silver rule).

And yet another little ditty for us to ponder pertaining to our tentative judgments as to how we shall deal which each person and situation we encounter on life's journey goes like this:

"You've got to know when to hold 'em.
Know when to fold 'em
Know when to walk away,
And know when to run."
(Lyrics from "The Gambler"
by Kenny Rogers)

❋　❋　❋　❋　❋

Ongoing Challenge

It is a part of the business of scientific inquiry to investigate into the realities behind appearances, to the extent that there exist adequate time, tools, and methods to accomplish such things. Philosophy is but a generalized form of knowledge that is dependent on scientific observation. It may be worthy of congratulations, in that it also implies **an effort toward an elevated vision with often honest intentions of acquiring wisdom.**

But Science is only a recent innovation in the history of mankind, and the tools and methods for the accomplishment of the task are only recently beginning to be evolved. The labors and difficulties of scientific-technological thought are only slowly evolving in our culture. It is said that perhaps 98 percent of all the professional scientists that have ever lived, are alive at this time. Another illustration of just how recent is the undertaking of scientific insight into the reality behind the elusive appearances of things.

It is unfortunately the case that we as individuals and as a society <u>presume to own much more truth and knowledge than what will ever eventually be established</u> as valid. And that having once acquired a body of misinformation and half-truths, we tend to be reluctant to abandon it, nor wholly willing to accept correction. In part, perhaps, because we have been to a great deal of pain and effort to gain possession of the material; and because of the work and effort of having to bend our thought processes to accommodate new information. <u>We develop a "certitude-of-belief" concerning that in which we have invested ourselves.</u> That certitude-of-belief becomes a great obstacle toward the advancement of human understanding. Would that we could be more modest, and could learn to be more pragmatic both individually and as a society. For we would be far better served to accept (what we presume to know) upon only a tentative basis. Our depth of understanding of the nature of reality certainly appears to have done little more than scratch the surface of that reality.

Finality

"In the long view, of course, one has no ultimate use for the personality, and needs must depart from it-as well as from this mortal flesh. And in departing, the things of consequence are: 1) the amount of truth that we have comprehended and endorsed to those within the sphere of our influence, 2) the inspiration which their memories of us, may have given (imparted) to them-to live a well-proportioned life of self-discipline, so as to encourage and enable them to see farther and more clearly than ourselves, and 3) that they continue to sally-forth into the universe of space-time on the wings of scientific advancement." (p. 157 *Fading Echoes*)

"Twas given to man ambiguous life,
Not so much blessing he,
As giving it the hope that there,
It might not wasted be.
RGB

Such evidence as exists, gives us cause to consider that we are each a transient fragment of a continuous and ongoing life, on an irreversible course through time and the universe. Though we are physically and physiologically different from our parents, sibling, and descendants, we would nevertheless be individually different even were we clones, because of the inevitability of our various life experience. And our response to that experience. The very fact of history confirms to us that ourselves and all things change under the influence of process and time. There is no reason to suppose that change, process, or time shall cease. There is even no science itself, apart from its ongoing change and advancement, based upon observations, experience, reason, and experimentation. Each race of creatures has its supreme gifts and abilities. Those of mankind include curiosity, memory, intelligence, reason, inventiveness. And a cultural tradition that accumulates, gathers, transmits, and applies knowledge and information to the living of our individual lives and advancement of civilization. So long as the necessary resources and opportunity are available to mankind, there is reason to expect that the frontiers of civilizations shall continue to advance into the universe. And the more so, as there is every reason to expect that there will be both resources and opportunity beyond the confines of planet earth. Since we expect that the universe will continue to show itself as a unity of interrelated parts with cause and effect relationships, we may hope that advancement of science and knowledge might gradually absolve its disjunction from moral philosophy.

When I breath my last breath, the agonies and satisfactions of my existence disappears forever into eternity. Even so, while I can yet endure, I cling to life as my sole ultimate possession.

In what respect would an afterlife be superior to blessed a non-existence?

Why does the bear go over the mountain? Is there something more to be seen than just the other side of the mountain?

Why(?), one might ask, do I trouble myself with all of these vexing and time consuming projects?

Because I have the health, the time, the curiosity and yet enough energy to do so. Because I have not yet learned how to sit quietly nor in blissful peace with myself in the sun. Because even an unwanted and essentially useless life might just as well be lived and endured with some little courage, energy, and hope; just as though it were of some significance. Because life challenges one to think. Because one must eventually charge oneself with the responsibility for discovering whatever he can of reality. Because a responsible adult being must ultimately define his own worthy agenda of life-even in the very act of living and enduring the agony of one's existence. We are but "inheritors of a few years and sorrows." And so I too must sit a spell to contemplate-beneath the Banyan tree.

Caesar's claim was, "Veni, Vedi, Vichi." (I came, I saw, I conquered) My own claim is less glorious. I came, I struggled, I pondered.

R. Garner Brasseur, M.D.

❉   ❉   ❉   ❉   ❉

Bibliography

Able, Reuben: *"Man Is The Measure"*: The Free Press, New York, 1976, ISBN 0-02-900140

Ashwell, Ken; *The Brain*; Firefly Books; James Mills-Hick, Publisher; Buffalo, NY; 2012; ISBN 978-1-77085-126-9

Bateson, Gregory: *"Mind and Nature"*; Bantam New Age Books; New York, N.Y. 1980; ISBN 0-553-1372-7

Berlinski David;, *"The Devils Delusion"*; Crown Forum, New York 2008 ISBN 978-0-307-39626-6

Blakemore, Colin: *"Mechanics of the Mind"*. Cambridge University Press; Cambridge England; 1977; ISBN 0 521 21558 5

Brasseur, R. Garner, M.D. *"A Studied Impression of That Which Is"*: *Vantage Press: New York*; 2006: ISBN:0-533-15365-4

Brasseur, R. Garner, M.D.; *"Fading Echoes"*; *Author House; Bloomington, IN; 2013; ISBN 978-1-4817-7161-1*)

Colapinto, John; "Brain Games" in *"The Best American Science and Nature Writing"* pp.73-96; *Houghton Mifflin Harcourt; Boston & New York 2010; ISBN 978-0-547-32784-6*

Durant, Will; *The Pleasures of Philosophy*; Simon and Schuster; New York, N.Y.; 1953

Dyson, Freeman, (Editor); *"Best American Science and Nature Writing"*: Houghton Mifflin Harcourt; Boston-New York; 2010; ISBN 978-0-547-32784-6

Gregory, R.L.; *Eye and Brain*; McGraw-Hill Book Company; New York Toronto; 1973: ISBN 0-07-024660-2

Husserl, Edmund: *The Idea of Phenomenology;* The Hague, Netherlands; Martinus Nijhofe; 1973; USBN 90 24701147

Halle, J. Louis: *Out of Chaos*; Houghton Mills; Jan 1977; ISBN 0395253578

Heaton, J.M.; *The Eye*; Travistock Publications; Distributed by J.B.Lippincott; Printed in Great Britain by The Camelot Press Ltd.; 1968

Huxley, Aldous; *The Doors of Perception: ISBN 10; 0080801714*

Hybrow, Peter W.,MD; *The Well-Tuned Brain*; W.W.Norton & Co.; NY: 2015; ISBN 978-0-393-07292-1

Krutch, Joseph Wood; *"The Measure of Man"*: Grosset's Universal Library; NY; 1954 ISBN: 54-6504

Marris, Emma; "I Marks the Spot"; *Discover Magazine*, December, 2014

McGowan, Kat: "The Second Coming of Sigmund Freud": Discover Mag. April 2014 pp.54-61

Michelet, Jules; Satanism and Witchcraft (translation by Allinson, A.R.); The Citadel Press; New York; 1939; ISBN 0-8065-0059-X

Meralo, Zeeya; "Tomorrow Never Was"; Discover

Magazine; June, 2015 pp.39-45.

Murchie, Guy; Music of the Spheres (in two volumes), by Dover Publications, Inc.; New York, N.Y.; 1967; ISBN 67-22255

Nedergaard, Helen & Colberg; Scientific American; March, 2016 p. 26

Parkinson, C. Northcote: *"Mrs. Parkinson's Law"*; Houghton Mifflin Co.: Boston, MA 1968

Pinker, Steven, *"The Stuff of Thought"*: Penguin Books, NY; 2008; ISBN 978-0-670-06327-7

Quiroga, Rodrigo Quian et al: "Brain Cells for Grandmother" *Scientific American*: February 2013: pp. 31-35

Rosenblum, Lawrence D.: "A Confederacy Of Senses": *Scientific American*: January 2013: pp. 73-75

Ryle, Gilbert, *"The Concept of Mind"*: Copyright 1949 Reprint Barns & Noble, Inc.; New York; 1969; L.C. number 59-14155

Smith, John E.; *"Philosophy of Religion"*; The McMillan Company, New York: 1965: Library of Congress number 65-11875

Taylor, A. E.; *"Socrates"; Double Day Anchor Books; 1953; ISBN 0883557185*

Tononi, Giullio and Cirelli, Chaiara: "Perchance to Prune": *Scientific American*: August 2013: pp. 34-39

Popkin, Richard and Stroll, Avrum: *"Philosophy Made Simple"*; Doubleday & Company, Inc.; Garden City, New York 1956

Rolf, Tamara L.; *"Satanism";* The Greenhaven Press in San Diego

Swift, Jonathan: *"Gulliver's Travels and Other Writings"*; Bantam Classic Edition; March 1981; New York, N.Y.; ISBN 0-553-21014-9

Willyard, Cassandra; *"Talking Heads";* Discover Magazine; July 23, 2015; p.22

Wilson, E.O.; "The Future of Life": Vintage Books, A Division of Random House, Inc., New York, March 2003 ISBN: 0-679-76811-4

Young, John K.; *Hunger, Thirst, Sex, and Sleep;* Rowan and Little Fields Publishes, Inc.; Lanham, Maryland; 2012